Memories
Of
Lockdown

First published in the United Kingdom in 2021 by
The Choir Press

ISBN: 978-1-78963-269-9

Cover design by Bob Hellyer
www.BobHellyer.art
Typesetting and layout by Phoenix Media
www.phoenixmediadesign.com

Thanks Mum & Dad
for your inspiration

Thank you for the Rose

"Thank you to my family and friends - without all
of you there would be no book"

Introduction

"I woke up one morning at the end of June 2021 and decided that I wanted to put a book together of "our lives during these times".

I had been watching families and friends becoming increasingly divided by their different views on what was going on in the world. People were suffering and if there was one thing we didn't need more of it was suffering.

We all have our own unique circumstances, views, beliefs, thoughts, feelings, hopes and fears and my aim for this book is to create more understanding, respect and love.

I have gathered individual heartfelt stories from my friends, ordinary people, of where they were in their lives when Covid struck and the world changed and how they have navigated the past 18 months.

The world is in crisis and we need unity, trust and love, not division, hopelessness and fear.

I have enjoyed reading the wonderful stories that have been shared with me and I hope you will too; I´ll see you again at the end of the book to say goodbye."

Rosanne

Rosanne

"My Story begins a few months before lockdown was announced........... I had been living with my elderly parents off and on for some time and when my Mum unexpectedly died at the end of November 2019 my world changed. My dearest and greatest friend had gone and I wasn't ready for it.

My parents were elderly but had always been well and had lived independently in the family home. The family had moved to West Sussex, because of my father's work in the August of 1959 when I was 4. They needed to buy a house and move the family that summer; they chose that house because it was ready to move into and decided to settle in and look around until a house they really wanted came up! They were to spend the next 60 years and the rest of their lives living there very happily.

Dad was left behind, the moment we never thought would happen had happened - Mum died first. She was so brilliant at organising everything but even she couldn't organise that - she would never have wanted to leave Dad, she would never have wanted him to suffer her loss. I am not sure which was greater, his loss or witnessing his loss. It was a terrible time.

We struggled through the next days and weeks, we made it through Christmas and I was able to visit Dad every day. Dad was in a beautiful Home where he and Mum had decided to go that October for 6 weeks to give Mum time to get well and to give them a chance to decide where they really wanted to be, as the realisation of not being able to live independently had arrived.

When they were making the decision to go into the Home for 6 weeks to get Mum back on her feet again and discussing finances, Mum said to Dad "let's think of it as the cruise we never had" - they had embarked on their new venture together with hope.

I watched the News with Dad every afternoon and from January onwards we found ourselves hearing and seeing the shocking news from Wuhan, the city being sealed off, people dropping dead in the streets and stories of some Brits not being able to get out and back to the UK.

Little did we know that within 2 months we would be facing the knock on effect across the world which would touch everyone in one way or another and our lives would never be the same again.

By mid- March I was told by the Home that I could no longer visit my Dad; my brain went into a spin. By the Friday I had discussed the situation with my family in Spain and made a plan to return home to them, before I couldn't, as Spain had announced they were locking down as from Sunday at midnight.

My reason for living in England was to see my Dad and if I couldn't see him then my reason had gone; with promises and a heavy heart I said goodbye to him on a telephone call and booked my flight to return to Spain.

I managed to book a flight for Sunday morning the 15th of March. I remember leaving the family home in the early hours, it was still dark, and as the taxi pulled away I looked up at my bedroom window thinking to myself "I never thought it would end like this".

I had walked beside my Mum as she left the house for the last time the previous September and beside my Dad as he left the house for the last time the previous October and now I was leaving anxious for the journey ahead and not knowing what the following days, weeks, months would bring.

We drove silently along quiet roads to Gatwick airport, I walked through an eerily deserted airport, no hustle and bustle, none of the usual airport buzz; people with their own worries, eyes down, walking past. I sat with 15 others in the departure lounge and boarded a plane with those same people.

People sat apart and the plane was quiet. At Alicante I expected to be thoroughly questioned as to why I was travelling and where I was going but no-one even looked at my passport. On the car journey home the roads were quiet, the roads I had grown to know and love were empty. I looked at the mountains on one side and the sea on the other side remembering all the happy times I had driven those roads with excitement going to and from the airport collecting family over the years, my children and my parents who had visited us so often.

During those first days being back in my lovely peaceful home I realized I could finally start grieving. I realized I had been given the "gift of time" and I was going to accept it gratefully and use it wisely.

We weren't allowed to leave our homes but it was no hardship for me as I didn't want to go anywhere or see anyone, my every step brought memories of happy times with Mum & Dad. They had been to view the house with us all those years before and most of the decisions we ever made over the years had been with their enthusiasm and encouragement - they were an integral part of our home.

The weather was miserable and we were all in a state of disbelief as to what had happened, and happened so fast.

I exchanged funny memes with my friends and we set up zoom calls - it was a little bit of fun for a very short time.

I spoke to Dad each day and he was in his wonderful wartime spirit of "making the best of things and just getting on with it" - it was heartwarming to hear his voice each day and I reassured him that I would return to England as soon as it was over and I could travel.

When, weeks later, it wasn't over and apparently I couldn't travel, and the news had announced that borders had closed I was not happy. Infact I was very unhappy because my eldest son and his partner and my Dad were in another country.

At 8 o'clock each night the ambulances and some police cars would noisily (as only the Spanish can) circle the local area so that we all had a chance to clap them - I did this for a while, always slightly bemused as to how so many of them were free and able to entertain us each evening in the height of a pandemic.

At this time in Spain there were many severe lockdown rules.

Children were not allowed out at all. If you had a dog you could walk around the block - up to 50m from your home I seem to remember. One member of the family could shop once a week at the supermarket closest to their home, not the supermarket of their choice.

I shopped for the family once a week and was regularly stopped by armed & masked police on the way to the supermarket and questioned. I also heard that people's bags were searched by  the police to see what they had bought in the supermarket; was it too much and could be considered panic shopping or was it not enough and they would have to shop more than once a week! Whichever way it was wrong!

After 7 weeks the children were allowed out with 1 parent (not both even though they all lived together) and for up to 1 km from their homes for 1 hour. What a relief to get the children into the fresh air!

A friend of mine walked to the beach with her children where they found the Cruz Roja (Red Cross) wandering around the beach giving out masks and the police patrolling this very small beach where mums and children were sitting apart. Children dipped their toes into the sea only to be told by the police that they couldn't and when one child did it again the policeman asked the mother for identification and when she didn't have it as she had only come down the beach for half an hour with her child, the policeman marched her and her child off the beach and said he would walk back to her nearby apartment with her to see her ID. At the last minute he didn't - she walked home alone. Safe to say mothers and children were duly traumatised.

It became apparent that I could start visiting my Dad again and so I started planning to return to England. Amidst all the "noise" of not being able to travel, I made my travel plans. Indeed, I could not fly from either of our local airports but I could fly from Barcelona and so in early June I left my home again. I was heavy hearted - always leaving family behind. However, the journey was smooth. The flight was good, a packed plane, very different from the one I had travelled out to Spain on just 3 months earlier at the beginning of lockdown, and the crew told me how they had flown daily throughout lockdown and the planes back and forth had been consistently full.

To see the world in crisis, people being divided in thought and belief was more than I could bear - literally. I had stopped watching the News many years ago when I couldn't bear to see the suffering of other people around the world in countries at war, disease, starvation; it was my self-preservation.

I have kept up to date with what's going on and have had times of getting involved in the noise when I found myself feeling strongly about something and couldn´t understand why others were not seeing things as I was.

Personally, to visit my elderly father weekly rather than daily was hard, but to not be able to hug him was heartbreaking and my heart broke a little more each time I left him.

Over the past months I have stepped back and observed more. I have learnt patience and trust and from the trust has come a calm which is wonderfully reassuring.

From the start of the first lockdown I have been grateful for the "Gift of Time". I can remember talking with my family in April/May 2020 and discussing how we could either become very depressed and intolerant during this time or face each day as it came and make the most of it and we unanimously chose to make the most of it!

I have inherited undaunted optimism from my father and unconditional love from my mother amongst many of their other virtues and the strength they gave me throughout my life has set me up well to deal with what we have now.

In their deaths my great depth of sadness has also taken me to a place of enormous gratitude for all they were, are, and always will be as my parents, and has so empowered me at a time when I need strength and brightness to make each day a good one. It would seem pointless to tackle each day in any other way."

Mark Watson

I live on the small Greek island of Patmos. I'm English, my wife is American. We have a 12 year old daughter who attends the local school and is kilometers ahead of us as a reader, speaker and writer of Greek. I teach online, I have done for over a decade; my wife is a functional medicine coach who also works on the net which made it possible for us to end up here. It was a choice to live somewhere we've always wanted to live. And when the pandemic struck it was a lucky choice.

I sat on the Internet monitoring what was happening in the rest of the world. I watched with growing horror and some personal trepidation at what was happening in England and the US. I heard from many that "it's just the flu" or "it's made up" and "it doesn't exist and it's a way for them to control us." But thought no, I thought, concluding from all I saw and read, this is something definitely real, definitely unpleasant.

So I kept in virtual contact with England, watched the numbers of deaths go up which saddened me – it's my country after all. I saw the lack of a well thought out government response, the fightback against the government's lack of response and I found myself thinking about World War II and how all England came together and accepted massive controls because they felt that this was for the better. I saw that spirit wasn't there, that there was huge polarization of opinions and nothing was breaching them. And the numbers of the dead kept going up.

Where I was, living and eventually because of the travel restrictions, stuck, on a small Greek island, there was the feeling of a firestorm brewing just over the horizon but that it wasn't reaching us. We knew it was there – out there – but I felt curiously geographically inoculated from it all.

And generally we were pretty safe, at least to begin with. The Greek government banned travel to and from the islands. There were only about 3000 people in total on the island and we were all spread out. All the same restrictions were dished out to us as for the rest of the country: about texting one of six reasons when you went out, shopping when you only had to and only then for food, having to wear a mask. (Which is where I heard my first joke of the whole pandemic from a friend of mine in Los Angeles undergoing the same restrictions, who told me they don't have to wear masks in LA because everyone's already wearing one.) The cafés and restaurants had closed so had the churches. But the disease never really got here in the first March to June lockdown of 2020. We still went for walks over the island on Saturdays, the texting thing dropped off, the police never really pushed things all that hard, my work was online which didn't change. We were safe basically from the disease – or as safe as you could be. And I started to feel privileged.

We were free relatively compared to a lot of what people were going through in England. We always had toilet paper in the shops. The boats were still running, the supermarkets were full so you would go shopping and it was a bit like, "Well, do we want to buy the avocados from Costa Rica, or the Mexican ones?" Privileged, as I say. But with nothing really happening and the world shut down it started to feel like we were in a cage – a gilded one to be sure, but still a cage. It was like we were in a prison but they'd given us the keys to our cell. We could go out but there was nowhere really to go. So we all went back inside at night having had our freedom but not being able to do anything with it.

I was concerned for myself about the virus. Some fear, but not a debilitating amount. Because of the not knowing if I was the one in the herd that this disease would thin out. I saw the mental and emotional toll this was taking on my sister and many friends in England, but I had something in my back pocket that helped to keep things calm. Having spent time on Mount Athos in the north of Greece with the monks, seeing their very different interpretation of Christianity – that God actually is love – and converting to Greek Orthodoxy, I always had a center of joy of comfort that I felt, that even if things went pear shaped, would never be lost. And it never was. That centre has held throughout.

There was a brief respite in the summer of 2020 when Greece opened up hoping to attract the tourist dollars. Few people arrived. No one from England. A few who travel independently or who have houses on the island got through, but none of our friends and the summer felt like strangely never having started.

We were free to move around though. We went on holiday to Karpathos and Leros. We started to see how pretty much across the board, business for the islands was down 30 – 70%. People were struggling. With my work and money coming in we could still pretty much live life as it was. I was in constant contact with my family and friends in the UK and I heard about the much stricter restrictions, and once more I felt privileged that we could do all this. I started to feel guilty about it too. There was England suffering and here was I lotus eating. I thought about World War

2 again and how all the English expats went back to help out. I thought about it but my going back would have only added to everyone's burden so I drank my retsina and ate my moussaka in empty restaurants and didn't feel entirely good about it. And then in October 2020 the second lockdown kicked in.

This one was harder lasting to May 2021. More people stayed: those that had houses or could work online. I remember going to a remote beach where the year before (2019) there had just been me, my daughter and a good friend of ours swimming at the end of November. This year there were 29 people on the beach. Only 4 of them were islanders. The rest were people from Belgium and France and Germany and Austria – most with houses – who figured out it was better to stay in Greece on an island than to go back home where nothing was open anyway.

Despite only renting a house, being in the company of these people I again felt privileged. Like somehow, by default we were in the same club – a bit like if Woody Allen at the beginning of Stardust Memories had managed to get onto the train with all the glamorous people. I spent the winter again, largely untouched by the disease, saw the horrible number of deaths in England going up and us still off on our weekend walks. And the guilt I felt started to feel like a strange kind of survivor's guilt.

We had a few cases over the years – not many, maybe 30. No one died, no one had to be helicoptered out due to our lack of a hospital here. Yet the horror stories from England continued. Our lives once more, by comparison, were so much better.

I considered not having the vaccine. But my age – 66 – and the fact that I'd been in England the Christmas before all this broke and I'd had some breathing problems made me very wary of this disease. I was in the same boat as everyone else – we didn't know whether we were the ones who would get this or not/get it badly or not/get long Covid or be ok. I remember talking to a friend of mine who suffers from Epstein-Barr and who said, whatever you do, "there is no golden choice here". She was right.

I wanted to do the AstraZeneca vaccine but it wasn't on offer here. In Greece the government made the decision to vaccinate all the islands first because that's where the money would be in terms of the following tourist season. I hesitated. But then I had a phone call with an old friend of mine in London from high school. He told me that his neighbour next door was overweight and unhealthy and had got the virus, suffered for a couple of weeks and was okay. Another neighbour was very fit, in his forties, got the disease and had been on a ventilator for 4 weeks. Over the other side of the road there was young woman in her twenties who had the virus, wasn't ill, but for the last year had had no sense of taste or smell.

I almost feel ashamed to say it but it was that last example that tipped the balance towards me getting the vaccine. I like food. I like tasting things and smelling roses and the cistus flowers here in the spring. So I did it and even this felt like a privileged decision – sort of like a rich person choosing one type of good wine over another– rather than a life or death one. At the time of the second shot, India was in turmoil - the death rate was skyrocketing. Knowing we were relatively safe and could have gone another 6 months without the vaccine, I wish I could have given mine to an Indian. But being white from the rich part of the world, our hands are always first in the cookie jar. The guilt really kicked in then. But, other than send money to those who needed help, I couldn't do much about it.

June 2021 came. England was still in hard-core lockdown. Travel was still virtually impossible. In the early part of the month I was in Kos dealing with some post Brexit paperwork. I was on a beach all by myself. I kept thinking about my friends in England who would love to be where I was but who couldn't be. In all my conversations with them I'd felt their weariness, their frustration, their growing hopelessness that this thing could go on forever and that normality would never return. I wanted to convey to them that there are still rays of Mediterranean light shining and one of them is shining for you.

I write poems occasionally. I wrote one with that and my friends in mind. It was called "It's All Still Here." And, well, yes it is. What was, still is, and it isn't going anywhere. The virus eventually will. It will be over. Even if there are another one, two, three more lockdowns. It wasn't much, but at that moment on that sunny beach, after months of not being able to do anythiing, it felt like it was something I could do. To share in a different way a little bit of Mediterranean sunshine that every morning I wake up to. As a privileged person who's very aware of how privileged they've been.

Julia Evans

I remember a couple of days before lockdown. I was sitting in my Studio painting. I was listening to Joy Division, and I was painting a clown! I had this idea for a Burlesque style collection of work but with a dark twist - think cabaret or creepy circus. I never did create that collection, maybe I will, writing this has reminded me......

Two of my girlfriends kept messaging me to go shopping, to "stock up". The type of girlfriends that are far more organised than me! The ones that always know what is going on at school and arrive on time with everything they need, perfectly in hand alongside a box of homemade cookies! They had been following the news with rigour and were already deep in the throws of a fear induced panic. I however had not been watching the news, I never do! Have not for over a decade! So was weighing up which was more important; painting a clown or "stocking up" for the impending apocalypse...... The clown was winning.

However my organised mum friends are somewhat feisty and insisted I go shopping with them. They pulled up at my door, it went something along the lines of "for f*** sake Julia just get in the car!" And off we went - just for the record I bought a normal quantity of toilet paper!. Thank God I did go, thank God I have friends that are like that and thank God they have a friend like me. We are all different and it is a combination of our different strengths when pulled together that allow us to move forward.

That is where it all began. Two or three days after that we were in lockdown..... possibly one of the best times of my life. Yes, I said it. I LOVED lockdown. Now I would like to point out that I live in a beautiful house with my art studio downstairs, I have a life full of abundance, cats and a large dog! I get on very well with my family, I am healthy and I love what I do. I live in a tiny Spanish village and my house backs onto the stunning Spanish countryside. I am lucky and brimming with gratitude everyday.

Gratitude, I will be talking about that a LOT. I have practiced the art of deep gratitude, along with radical self responsibility, meditation and many other great tools for many, many years. I have used these tools to create a beautiful life. It was these tools, a general love of life, plus my practice in Art that allowed me to LOVE my lockdown experience and use it to my advantage.

Now that is not to say that I was dancing on unicorn dust for the whole time. Through Lockdown I faced one of my biggest fears. Money. Or not having enough money to support my family.

You see I am a single Mum and financially support both of my children alone. I do this through a successful yet small Art-based business, teaching classes and workshops from my Studio.

When lockdown hit my business was thriving, the best it had ever been. With full Art classes and a waiting list. I was on the verge of expanding into Art holidays. I had nurtured this business for over twelve years, built it from nothing,  and overnight my business, my baby, was killed. Swiped clean out at the knees. I will also say that finance is not one of my strong points. I had enough money saved to get us through for about six weeks. I was just about to receive some advanced payments for future workshops that had to be cancelled. My capacity to earn easily had been taken away along with all I had built. It was heartbreaking.

I was gripped with fear. It was suffocating. I had the weight of having to support two children on my shoulders. In truth I was terrified. I knew I had the capacity to earn money in other ways, I am constantly making plans for the future. But I also knew that most of those plans would take time, more time than I thought I had and money. I was terrified, I was paralysed with fear.

This is where years of personal development came into play, and also why I am a huge advocate of working on yourself and learning the tools to get yourself out of any situation. The first thing I knew that I needed to do was work on my mindset. I knew that I could not get us through this when my mind, body and soul were held in the harsh hands of terror.

The first thing I did - I meditated, yes that is right! I did not start panic planning or working on strategies. I went into deep meditation. The second - a gratitude practice. Now I could write for hours on this alone but that is for another day. I will say that through a spiritual practice I managed to release my fear and began to think clearly within a day or two. It is what I describe as emotional toughness, a way that you can work through emotions quickly without ignoring them and turn them around. I meditated everyday in lockdown and I said silent prayers of gratitude with every step I took.

This made me see my life from a very different perspective, we had so much abundance, life was beautiful, I have always felt this but I knew I needed to take it to a whole new level. And within this stunning vibration I created "The Unshakable Artist." I had been playing with the idea of building an online education platform for some time. I was planing to get a professional website designer and film maker to help me build it. I have built websites and had some video skills but nothing of that level. I knew that I did not have the budget nor the full skill set or access to the professionals I was planning to work with. However I focused on what I did have. A great computer, a smart phone, the internet, the capacity to learn - we can always learn, and TIME.

I had the time to do it. In truth if it had not been for lockdown I would never have built what I did, my business would have stayed where it was for many years, I would never have had the courage to close it down for two months and build a new part to the business. I believed that I always had to run a certain amount of classes to earn enough - this was a belief not a truth and having my hand forced showed me this. In fact lockdown showed me many truths.

I am a bit of an obsessive workaholic but I was shown that there is a different way to do things.

After a couple of weeks I began to feel deeply rested. Now I was working a lot BUT I did not have to stick to appointments. In general life between work, kids and family there is somewhere I need to be everyday. This is exhausting. Being with people so much is exhausting. I was forced to stop and for the first time since being a mum, fourteen years, I felt rested.

Lockdown had allowed me to set my own hours and it felt that there were so many hours in a day. I could spend time with my children, I could stop for lunch, I could snuggle and play and still have plenty of time left to work.

I loved what I was building so much that I was waking up everyday full of excitement. Many found it hard to get motivated but I was under pressure to create an income and because of the constant gratitude and meditation, the stress did not get to me - most of the time!

It is not to say that I did not have my moments but I always managed to get my mindset back to the idea that this was not a curse but a gift.

The Gift of Time.

I did it, I recorded and edited over 150 video tutorials, built a learning platform, created a wonderful online community that I know helped and served many others. When we hold the power to help and serve at the forefront of a business idea it will nearly always lead to success. I was able to motivate and inspire from the comfort of my own home and now am able to reach a much wider audience than I ever could before. I managed to earn, to pay the rent, the bills and put food in the fridge.

As I write these words it has been over eighteen months since this journey began and I can honestly say that I am different person.

We all have so many plans and goals for the future, I know that my business would never have evolved if I had not been given the gift of lockdown.

I faced my biggest fears and realised that I could get through it. Now I have a whole new source of income and my business is better that ever. I have also evolved spiritually and as a person.

Looking back I do think - "Julia how the hell did you do that". And in truth I put my trust in the Universe and raised my vibration. When we can do this we have the power to do anything. And always, always be thankful, deeply thankful for what you do have.

2020 was tough, no doubt about it, but in amongst the tough times we had some amazing times. I have some beautiful family memories from lockdown and I connected with my loved ones on such a deep level. We are wired to focus and magnify the negative things in our lives. There is nothing wrong with that. We are wired that way for our survival. Once upon a time a negative thing would have been being eaten by a wild animal!

We could be faced with 9 positives and one negative and we will naturally focus on that one negative. That is how we are made.

The last eighteen months have been full of ups and downs. I had to close the Studio again earlier this year, just as I had got it up and running again.

I know there are so many out there who have it much worse than me at the moment but I am still surrounded by magical moments, lots of little beautiful things and I have no doubt there will be more, lots more........

One thing I do know is what we focus on grows and when we learn to focus on what we do have that will grow.

From a seed of Gratitude you will be surprised at what can grow.......

Kat

Stay Wild, Moon Child

Wild was indeed how I felt when lockdown mark 1 was announced. I didn't yet have the scientific terminology to back up why I felt so livid and disillusioned ~ but I knew in my gut that this wasn't right.

We humans don't listen to our gut enough, we delegate to what we perceive as the superior authority, our overly complex brains. Evolution gave us that "gut feeling" as an instant protective mechanism, it's served me well over the last 18 months. I know it's 18 months because I make and wear a new friendship bracelet for every month that this farce goes on for.

Of course when PM Johnson (I refuse to call him "Boris", he is not my buddy) initially said "it's just 3 weeks" I decided to do a bracelet per week. I'd now be on... circa 68 of them and probably limiting the blood supply to my hands so I too had to "follow the science" and change my policy to a monthly lockdown bracelet. That was one of my "coping mechanisms" - a little bodily  visual tally like prisoners do in their cells. Because I do feel like a prisoner, after all, we've all been told we're not allowed to have our freedom and autonomy. The democratically elected government has decreed this based on shadowy meetings conducted behind closed doors with people who have a vested interest in lockdowns and pharmaceuticals. They told us we can't hug or even see the people we love. That we have to cover our faces because that reminds us that we are supposed to fearful.

I don't wear an obedience muzzle though - you may have sensed this already. These 18 months have been my greatest challenge but I know I'm stronger than ever. The first few times I went bare faced into a supermarket defying the illogical "science", I won't lie, my heart was racing. Now I wouldn't think twice about it and I'm proud to say that my children have never ever seen me in a mask. I couldn't bear them to think of me that way - I want to raise strong, independent free thinkers who are capable and confident enough to question those who presume authority. I remember nudging (she may say pushed) the eldest off one of those ridiculous 2m social distancing spots that are scarring our town centres. "We don't stand on colourful spots because the government tells us to" I announced. She's never done it again!

My other coping mechanism has been exercise. I have run more than I've ever done in my life. And when I wasn't running I was religiously doing press-ups. There is no more accommodating a companion to take your frustrations out on than the pavement.

I also decided that to help me break free from inane diktats, that I needed to do something slightly off piste and unpredictable. So I set out getting my motorbike licence and then a rather snazzy Kawasaki. It gave me focus (its hard taking a driving test at 39)  and makes me feel empowered. My daughters ask why I can't just bake cakes like "normal mothers". I tell them it's important to aim higher than "Normal".

I fly for a living - it's been an interesting time in aviation. Despite what people think, I've kept flying throughout. It's been amazing to see other countries and to appreciate that - actually - no where in the world is suffering the zombie apocalypse.

India gets told we are. We get told India are. Repeat.

One of my favourite stories is when I needed a plumber to come round. They called the day before to ask me the obligatory COVID questions. I was in a slightly obstreperous mood so when he asked

"Have you been anywhere international in the last 3 months?" I decided to answer with the whole truth and nothing but the truth…

"Yes!" I said, "are you ready?".

Slightly nervous "Yes" resonates down the phone.

"I've been to… Barbados, Mauritius, Tel Aviv, Boston, Seattle twice, Hong Kong three times and oh I'm sure I'm forgetting one… ah yes, Lima, Peru."

There was a slight pause as one might expect and then he said "But you feel alright in yourself right?".

"Yes I feel perfect thanks".

"Great, see you tomorrow." And that I believe is how the pragmatic among us have been getting on with life and ignoring most of the nonsense Downing Street try to shower us with.

Now to deal with the traumatic experience that was home schooling. I have two daughters and they were in Reception and Prep 2. Any Mum or Dad that has endured this will know how truly awful this experience was for… well… everyone. The eldest wants to be an astronaut and is her harshest critic. The youngest is naturally charming and I believe has an innate ability to land on her feet whilst maintaining a carefree smile, which is a long winded way of saying that the eldest occupied most of my time and effort whilst the little one got away with doing a lot of jigsaws.

In the end, force feeding the National Curriculum down their throats became so onerous that we all but ditched it. I then taught them about volcanoes, Queen Victoria, Pandora's box, penguins and anything they showed an interest in. If you asked either of them what they remember from homeschooling they'd bring up "Medusa". Drawing a picture of a Greek icon with snakes for hair obviously affects primary school children!

My other major achievement was inadvertently teaching the 5 year old to mash up my swear words. I hope other parents can empathise that during lockdown schooling the odd swear word might have slipped out at particularly frustrating moments - like the eldest telling me they "DON'T DO TIMES TABLES LIKE THAT ANYMORE". Whilst I'm prepared to accept that methods have changed with phonics and long division, I would maintain that times tables are fairly set in stone as a system. So, during this period my two favoured swear words were the occasional "fuck" and "oh bugger". Once, whilst colouring in a picture, the 5 year old dropped her crayon. There was a small pause whilst she thought of the appropriate word, then she very proudly - and with some venom - settled on "OH FUCKERS!" I just had to leave the room and snigger, she still does it occasionally but I don't have the heart to tell her off. Sometimes life IS just a bit oh fuckers, even when you're 5 and all that's happened is you've dropped a crayon.

The other classic lockdown cliche I found myself having to adapt to was Living With The Ex (the father of our wonderful children). We decided that it would be better to keep the status quo and ride out lockdown #1. It's only 3 weeks after all! Oh wait. It's a few months. Christmas. Easter. Summer. This Christmas. Next summer. Hang on what year is it? Do you ever forget what year it is? I regularly think to myself "covid NINETEEN…so that was 2019 so it must now be 2020. We can't possibly have been doing this for years plural…" In light of the lockdown gift that keeps giving The Ex bit the bullet and did eventually move out. I actually felt quite melancholy about it, despite being completely emotionally apart we are allies in the covid narrative and have always agreed that the children will never get jabbed. There's a formidable brick wall of Mums and Dads who feel this way, PM Johnson is going to get concussion when he bulldozes headlong into us. Threatening me with nightclubs, pubs and travel I find vaguely amusing and slightly desperate but, come for my children, and I shall release the Tiger Mum.

I found that a good way to boost my morale and embrace my inner Tiger was to join the occasional Freedom March in London. They made me realise that not only was I not alone, but I was in a substantial minority. If 1.5 million freedom fighters can be deemed a minority? All ages, all walks of life, all careers, all races, all backgrounds, all carrying different hopes, dreams and worries. I even saw two children on their rollerblades. I would come home invigorated that although I've lost a good few friends to the COVID orthodoxy, I've gained just as many and we've all been on a similar journey of disbelief at what has happened to our country and the world.

I could never have guessed that terminology such as epidemiologist, spike proteins, myocarditis, lipids, mRNA, ivermectin and adenovirus would become a regular and comfortable part of my lingo. That I could write SARS-CoV-2 and know without pause which letters are capitalised. Hours of deep internet research diving has given me the knowledge to intelligently support my original wildly instinctive reaction. My brain and gut are in happy harmony with each other, which is why, despite this charade going on ad infinitum, I feel better than a year ago when my journey began. But what of that other essential organ, the heart? Well I try to stay hopeful that this dismal period in history will end, that love will triumph no matter what weird "Normal" we find ourselves in. Because Good Vs Evil is the perpetual human story is it not? In the western world we have been cushioned from this and forgotten that men will always hunger for power and money. We've been too busy with first world problems like worrying about pronouns and the correct angle to hold our phones when taking selfie's so we look slim.

I hope anyone reading this and everyone I know - including my wonderful friends who find me too prickly to be around (why won't she just tow the damn line!) realise that no one can dictate how you live your life and how you manage your own health. One of the greatest cons of this debacle is that you have to take an experimental medical substance in order to garner back your freedoms.

Stay Wild. Moon Child.

Kate from Languedoc, South of France

A few years ago I moved to the Languedoc region of France with my husband Adrian and his Japanese mother Sonoko.

We've been running a busy B&B here whilst looking after Sonoko during her decline into the final years of dementia. She passed away last year which I will touch upon later.

I think, as with most people, the first reports I heard about Covid did not concern me overmuch. Numerous viruses have come and gone in recent years in other parts of the world without making too much of an impact globally, but as time went on, the news became more and more alarming as the situation quickly became really serious in Italy. We are used to hearing about epidemics in the Far East and Africa so for us westerners it was a shock to hear about such an enormous death toll in Europe.

As I have family and close friends in the UK, I was keen to keep abreast of how things were unfolding there and it was incredible to see the cavalier attitude of the UK government in comparison to the European and other world leaders.

By March, the prospect of a total lockdown was approaching, with a few preliminary steps such as the closing of schools and borders. The fateful day came on the 17th March. At the time, we weren't unduly worried as we saw this as a very temporary situation which would last a month at the most and would act as a kind of firebreak. In the event it lasted until 11th May.

As we were preoccupied with our usual winter/spring renovation and redecoration activities, we both saw this as an advantage and made plans to use the time and embark on more ambitious projects in the knowledge that we would not be receiving any guests for a while. It felt odd and unpleasant to have to account for any outings from the house by filling in an "attestation" form, stating the purpose and duration of one's activity.Only essential trips being allowed.

The Orwellian nightmare of having someone breathing down one's neck! However, as we live deep in the countryside, we did escape on foot into the hills for sanity walks, in the knowledge that we would not run into any officials! These daily sorties into nature definitely helped to keep us,and our dogs, sane. This first lockdown coincided with wild asparagus season and I will never again go foraging without thinking of that surreal time and the conversations we had about our new mode of existence. This initial stage was definitely a time of reflection and reassessment of the important things in life. I came to realise what an integral part nature and wild spaces play in my life and how healing it is to spend time deep in its embrace. During the early stages of Covid it was easy to forget that some things do carry on as if nothing has happened, and nature is a good example of that.

We recognised how incredibly fortunate we were in comparison to many people around the world and often reflected on this fact. Watching Channel 4 news every evening was a painful experience as the sheer horror of world events became apparent. The poor families shut up in small apartments with no outside space and children climbing the walls. The harassed parents trying to work from home and keep their children occupied/educated at the same time. The people who have lost businesses or found themselves without any income. The refrigerated lorries parked up outside New York hospitals to store the ever-increasing amount of corpses, each one a precious loved-one, now being treated like dead cattle. The dreadful footage coming out of the Italian hospitals of people fighting for breath in corridors and turned onto their bellies to try to ease the pressure in their lungs.

Not to mention, all the people whose lives were pretty intolerable before the pandemic hit - people living in extreme poverty, or in refugee camps; people living in war zones etc. All of their lives have been made that much worse by this hellish situation. It was very humbling and somewhat uncomfortable to be in a position where our only suffering was down to the minor inconveniences of life under lockdown and the mounting anxiety of what the future would bring.

At this time, Adrian's mother Sonoko had reached the final stages of her dementia and was requiring a lot of care. We had two wonderful male nurses who came morning and evening as well as a rotation of carers who came at lunchtime to feed her and sit with her. It was from these people that we received our regular updates on the situation locally. It was apparent that they were extremely concerned and anxious, especially when we saw the meticulous preparations they made before entering Sonoko's room. They would not even accept the offerings of cakes and biscuits I used to give them in recognition of their kindness and patience. When Sonoko finally passed away in August of 2020, she spent her last 24 hours in hospital and Adrian was only allowed to visit her briefly. Her funeral was a small affair and our closest friends here were unable to attend due to having to self-isolate. Adrian's sister was unable to come from the UK and was understandably very distressed by this.

As I speak daily to my sister in the UK, I also became aware of how lucky we are in France to have such an outstanding healthcare system. At no point did I encounter any difficulty in seeing my GP or accessing dental care. A very different story for my sister who has had various health issues and has basically been completely neglected, a situation which worries me enormously. I am not blaming the NHS for this... but the appallingly incompetent government for their cuts and lack of support for doctors and nurses. As well as the excellent healthcare, we felt very supported financially by the French government and only had to submit our previous years' income for the months of lockdown, to be fully reimbursed. Again, we felt extremely privileged. Our taxes here are high, but we feel the system works very well as a result.

With regards to my worries about catching the virus, I have to say, I was not at all concerned. Case numbers were so low in our region, it was highly unlikely that we would come into contact with anyone carrying it. My son Benny, who lives in Canada with his girlfriend Emily, did catch it but they were not too badly affected. It was alarming to hear they had tested positive but far worse than that was when Emily found a lump on her breast and subsequently went through a double mastectomy. It was utterly dreadful to not be able to support them and to not be able to hug Benny when he was in tears on the phone. I was also very worried about my family in the UK, especially my nephew who was cooped up in a flat in London, where cases were increasing alarmingly. Luckily, he and his girlfriend have managed to avoid catching it so far.

As the restrictions started to be relaxed in May 2020, a few bookings trickled in, but our whole modus operandi had to change and it was very stressful having to wear masks and keep everything sanitised in the house. Room changes took a lot longer with all surfaces having to be sterilised and we started washing the linen at higher temperatures.

Before the pandemic, we had made a lot of changes and were about to launch a buffet breakfast where guests could take a tray, help themselves to their breakfast and sit where they wanted. We had invested in new fridges and various other items which of course, for now, can't be used. We were also on the verge of launching a lunch-club to non-guests. In fact we had just published the first date and had had a great response when the lockdown was announced. We had become keen to expand our business and do more catering so we had invested in new kitchen equipment, all of which was rather bad timing. Having said that, the two summers we've had since this bizarre time started have in fact been busier than usual, especially this year, 2021. Last year we only had French guests but this year we have had Belgian, Dutch and German guests so it's interesting to see the changing face of the pandemic in this way.

We have managed to escape over the border to Spain a few times, most recently at the beginning of July. We go to the same campsite and have noticed some changes in behaviour; the most striking being the almost complete lack of masks this time compared to the last time, in October 2020, when people were even wearing them on the beaches. These little breaks have been a real tonic and seeing the more relaxed approach recently was reassuring Although we only venture a couple of hours' drive from home, it

feels like a wonderful change of scene - again we so appreciate that we can do this.

Adrian and I have both had two jabs and although I was a little worried about having the vaccine, I am now glad to have had it with no ill-effects, so far, as it means I can travel more freely and also reassure our guests. I am very conflicted over the issue of compliance and obligation to get the vaccine. I hate the idea of vaccine passes and obligatory jabs for certain workers but I am also desperate for us to get the numbers down and to return to normality, especially for the children who's lives have been stopped in their tracks. I have spoken to several doctors who have been staying here as guests and they are all of the opinion that it is safe and the only way we will see an end to this situation. They have all had the jab without a moment's hesitation and one of them explained to me in detail how this vaccine differs entirely from the ones in the past which had long experimental phases. The make up of this one apparently prevents it from causing long-term effects. There will be a tiny percentage of people who have bad side-effects, some even resulting in death but compared to the Covid death-toll this is negligible.

My first grandchild was born in March '21. My son Luke moved over here three years ago and lives just up the road with his girlfriend Jo, her 7 yr old daughter Gemma and now little baby Willow has appeared, much to my delight. I am so happy that they are close by and I can see them regularly. At the time she was born, Luke was terrified that he wouldn´t be allowed to be present at the birth, or would be ejected from the hospital just after. In the event, he stayed there for two days after Willow was born and all was well. She has brought so much joy into our lives at a time when we all needed a boost, but for Luke the happiness is tinged with the regret that none of his family can meet her yet. Benny was meant to be coming from Canada for two weeks in August but has had to cancel, as has Luke's dad.

For me, the biggest sadness is not seeing my sister who I am very close to. I was really hoping to get back to the UK last autumn, then again in the spring of this year, but keep being disappointed. The inconsistency of information is unbelievable and must be piling stress onto stress for so many people. I still hope to be able to make a trip this autumn but in the new "what will be, will be" attitude that everyone is now having to adopt, I will just have to wait and see.

There are times when everything feels rather apocalyptic. The combination of Covid and climate change with it's now all too apparent effects being felt globally make the world seem a very hostile place to be living in. With the fact that us humans have brought this all upon ourselves, it's hard not to see this mayhem as some kind of divine judgement. Let's hope for the sake of our children and grandchildren that the world population is coming to its senses in time.

So for now, the world holds its breath as we all join together in the hope that this will all pass, one way or another and we will get back to doing all the things we love, especially spending time close to our loved ones, hugging, kissing, dancing and all mask-free!
My initial hopes that this time of reflection and suffering would improve the human condition seem not to have come to fruition with more conflict and intolerance than ever erupting around the world. Let's hope that our mutual grief and pain will engender more compassion for our fellow travellers on this journey.

Graham – "The Prescription Story"

Needing a repeat supply of eye drops I took the prescription to the surgery and not wanting to disturb the rather fractious lady in the Reception office I placed my repeat prescription in the box provided.

"What are you doing?" came a furious voice behind me.

"Just putting this prescription in the box as usual" I said.

"You can't do that!" She bellowed.

"It's no problem" I said, "I've just done it".

"Prescriptions don't go in there" she insisted.

"I think they do" I pointed out, "the sign says Put your prescription in box"

"That was before covid obviously" she ranted, "you have to put it in the letterbox outside."

"Ok" I said, "I'll take it out of the box and go outside to put it in the letterbox."

"You can't touch it now, just leave it and I will have to remove it" she said with the furious resignation of someone who has been told they must scale Everest blindfolded.

I thanked her profusely and left.

Shortly after, the consultant gave me additional eye drops to be taken twice daily without fail. The small bottle is not transparent so one doesn't know when it will run out..normally they last about 1 month. Mine ran out after 3 weeks. With trepidation I returned to the surgery which by now had a locked door and appointment only regime so I buzzed the intercom in the foyer and requested an urgent prescription so I could avoid missing the vital daily drops.

"We can't discuss anything medical over the intercom" came the exasperated response.

"I think we can" I explained, "as I can't get in as the door is locked, you are the surgery staff, I am the patient, the eye drops are for me and there is no one else here to overhear us" - which I thought was a good point.

"You have to put it in writing" she insisted, "so the doctor can consider it."

"But you've got the consultant's letter on your file" I said! This I thought was my trump card!

"YOU have to put it in writing" she insisted.

"I don't have pen or paper" I said!

"Use the pen and paper on the table behind you" she snarled.

I picked up the only sheet of paper...problem.

Intercom again, "Yes what is it?"

"The printed sheet of paper says... only use this if you are pregnant...and I don't think I am".

"Ignore that and write on the back"

"But what if a pregnant person arrives, she will have no form?"

"Just write on the back"

Intercom. "OK, I've written a note for the doctor, will you come and get it?"

"No, just put it in the letterbox".

"What shall I do then, wait?"

"Yes wait, we will tell you what the doctor says".

10 mins later.Intercom."I'm still here, what did the doctor say, can I get the urgent drops?"

"Don't wait here, wait at home!"

Sadly it's only after the event that I realised I should have said, haven't I seen you on Fawlty Towers, but given my age and inevitable future medical needs no doubt further opportunities lie ahead!

Cathy

For me Lockdown has been beneficial in so many ways, in fact my list of good things that came out of it is definitely considerable. To begin with I had far more time with my teenagers than I ever would have dreamt of having in 'normal' times. I worked from home so there was no hectic commute to navigate which was such a treat. My spare time was spent cooking for the bottomless pit appetites teenagers have! Fortunately I like cooking and had built a comfortable recipe corner in my kitchen hosting all my cooking books, a floor lamp, an armchair and a table for the book I might choose to peruse for the next feast. I tried all sorts of new meals and greatly enjoyed exploring new recipes. Some nights I definitely didn't feel like cooking until I remembered what else was I going to do, ie we couldn't go out for dinner so I just got on with cooking and seeing it as my evening entertainment.

I can't stress how much cooking I did often making two

breakfasts, two lunches and even two dinners. I once made a lasagna thinking that would be good and my lad said thanks for the snack, what's for dinner? On Christmas day I actually downed tools and after two evening meals said it was over to Domino´s to keep you alive until tomorrow. After all that festive food which is not known for being light to digest by any means they actually ordered a pizza that night!

As you can imagine much of the time was spent in the kitchen, though with the fabulous weather and a good wifi signal I was able to sit and work in the garden too. Oh and speaking of kitchens I was just grateful to have one, had Lockdown happened any earlier I would have been knee deep in renovations. In fact at one stage all I had functioning was a Kettle, otherwise there was no fridge, no cooking facilities, no heating, no hot water (I was going to the gym for showers), no working bathrooms...can you imagine if Lockdown had hit during that phase? In other words I spent every day in Lockdown counting my blessings that it had happened when it did because the house was by then comfortable and comparatively habitable.

As ever with renovating a house there were (and still are!) plenty of snagging jobs to tend to and without the stress of the commute and being home during my work day lunch hour, I was able to push further renovations through at break neck speed and to be home for builders to come and quote, another benefit. I've also been able to take the dog on much longer walks which we have both enjoyed immensely. In other words Lockdown brought us so many positive outcomes.

An unexpected benefit was all the money I saved by not being able to spend it, though as already indicated my food budget somewhat exploded. Also, I realised I don't need much and this is a lasting result in my purchasing decisions going forward on 'nice to have' things like too many pairs of shoes. I think I wore my trainers throughout. In fact I went on a date when we were out of Lockdown and threw on a pair of heels I had previously comfortably danced the night away at a party in Dubai until 3 in the morning. They were wedges so they were 'comfortable' but I was so out of practice wearing them I could barely walk on my date which was beyond embarrassing, needless to say there wasn't a further date! I blame the shoes, not my great company :)! I do wonder if the global demand for heels has crashed? I now buy funky coloured trainers as my replacement for having nice fun shoes.

Unlike most people I know, I didn't spend any of my evenings binge watching Netflix or opening a bottle of Wine. My routine was mostly working from home, cooking, taking the dog for a nice walk, more cooking and when in bed perhaps listening to an informative or inspirational documentary. Life felt on the whole very calm. I didn't watch any of the news so unlike most I wasn't in a fear frenzy. A friend remarked you know your life is a certain way when Lockdown makes no difference to it and she went on to say she loved Lockdown as there was no pressure to do things, particularly when she would rather not do them. It was funnier than that but you get the gist.

As for the reason behind putting us in Lockdown I have been skeptical throughout. If it were a pandemic surely I, and most people I know, would know someone who has died and I don't, nor do they. If for example you had 300 people in a room and asked them who has been affected by Cancer to stand up, we'd all stand up, I'd stand up about 15 times. If we asked the same room of people who has been affected by Covid I imagine the majority would sit down. We all know the story of the neighbour's cousin's postman's dog sitter's nan who might have had it but that is as close as it gets. I have friends who have worn masks, do tests several times a week, have had the jabs and they've self isolated countless times. I haven't done any of those things, not been sick once and never had to self isolate, is there perhaps a link?

In my view the numbers were initially inflated until the tests came out when they could increase those numbers as 'cases'. There are plenty of people who have tested positive and they are absolutely fine but they count as a 'case'.

Also while Lockdown has been positive for us there are far too many people who it has been detrimental to, I am thinking of those with mental health issues, people in domestic violence situations, people living on their own etc., in fact I suspect the cost of keeping us in Lockdown was far greater than it would have been if we just carried on while encouraging the vulnerable to look after their health and take the necessary precautions they needed.

I honestly think Lockdown has proved we are so gullible. I mean if I had gone to my Doctor 2 years ago and said I'd like to be tested for Spinal Meningitis and my Doctor said well what are your presenting symptoms and I said I don't have any but I want to be tested, and in fact have everyone I've been in contact tested too and so on, my Doctor would have thought I was a nutter and yet here we are constantly testing people without symptoms. How serious can a disease be if you have to be tested to know you even have it?

A Doctor friend told me he was not allowed to perform any surgeries during Lockdown as they didn't want to have patients exposed to Covid in hospitals. Now there is a huge backlog of people needing procedures and having to wait for them, myself included. What will be the health cost of that for people? Of all the things in Lockdown I'd say this is the main cost to me personally and to many others.

To be honest one of the points I don't understand is why people want to take a jab, it's not a vaccine as it doesn't prevent Covid and a vaccine by definition should prevent a disease. The jabs are in clinical trials, ie you are being a guinea pig having it. Plus there is a 99% + recovery rate from what is being labeled Covid (I suspect it's the flu rebranded) so why take an unknown risk putting something into your body? If you look at the ingredients they read like a Steven King horror. We'd all be much better off and healthier with fresh air, exercise, getting into nature, taking helpful supplements and hugging our loved ones, funnily enough most of the things we were advised not to do!

As for the mandates, these go against basic human rights established in things like the Nuremburg Code post World War 2, the Universal Declaration of Human rights, the Magna Carta, the Bill of Rights and other International Conventions...no-one has the legal right to tell you what to put in your body. Body integrity is a fundamental tenant of Law so it will be interesting to see the legal challenges that will likely unfold in due course. I wish people were more aware of their basic rights and less somewhat mindlessly gripped by the headlines fed to them via the media!

Jack

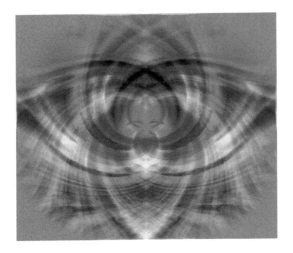

Over the past 18 months in England I have lived with government guidelines and lockdowns.

I have worn a mask to cover my nose and mouth.

I have stayed at a 2m distance from another human.

I have walked on pavements with painted footprints to tell me which side of the street I could walk on and which direction I could walk in.

I have queued to get into supermarkets.

I have sat on pavements drinking take away coffee because I am not allowed to sit inside a cafe.

I have witnessed people dodge each other to avoid human contact.

I have seen people driving alone in their cars wearing masks.

I have heard numerous stories from people unable to see their doctor because their local surgery is closed; they can only book a phone call with their doctor.

I have seen and heard relentless reminders of what I can´t do because of the pandemic, constant supermarket announcements, constant announcements when I travel on the train.

I have watched endless advertisements on the tv with scary news and pictures.

I have seen politicians not following the rules they set for us.

I have never heard or seen anything to reassure me, to make me feel remotely safe during this pandemic.

I have seen and heard new rules being announced, panic, panic, and then changed.

I have been encouraged to get the vaccine by members of the royal family, celebrities and politicians.

I followed all of these guidelines and gave up time with my family. Will my sacrifices have made all the difference and we will all go back to normal?

What will happen over the next 18 months?

Anne

My first memory of note was a lunch time meet I had with my 29 year old son in London on 10th March 2020. We met in the Crypt café underneath St Martins in the Field in Trafalgar Square. A favourite spot.

I had been visiting my family on the south coast of England and we met for lunch as I passed through London on my way home to south Wales.

My son works in the international news industry and was very up to date on what was happening globally as well as in the UK with the virus. I was not.

I had been out of the country for much of the preceding month on holiday in Malaysia – I remember that when we flew out to Malaysia in early February we were literally heading towards the virus as it was ripping through China and east Asia and then by the time we returned to the UK in March, CV-19 (as it was first termed) had arrived on European shores and we were soon to see those shocking images of hospitals in northern Italy struggling to cope with the onslaught of patients sick with this deadly respiratory virus.

Back to the lunch time meet with my son…. he advised me that what was about to happen to us in the UK now the virus was here was unprecedented, that despite my 3+ score years I probably had not seen anything like what was about to happen – had I?

How right he was – none of us had experienced anything like this before and we were and still are, in uncharted territory.

As time went on and the first lockdown was announced less than two weeks later on the 23rd March I remember being terrified that Boris Johnson and his cabinet of Brexiters – chosen for their support for Brexit rather than their competences – would be in charge of things that would have a direct impact on me and my family and friend's health and survival. How did we end up with such a buffoon running our government? Politically in the UK the results of the Referendum caused havoc and for the three plus years preceding the pandemic we were in total disarray as a country. We were not in a strong place to be dealing with a global pandemic. How grateful I was at this time to see Boris flanked by Chris Whitty and Patrick Vallance at the nightly Downing Street press conferences – at least our PM was listening to the advice of scientists who knew what they were talking about.

Boris' own brush with Covid was upsetting – when he was taken into intensive care in April the country was on tenterhooks. I was of course pleased that he survived but also pleased that he would surely now have to take this pandemic seriously and not listen to any whacky ideas coming from his unelected Vote Leave advisers including Dominic Cummings.

Cummings of course is now discredited and although I have

no doubt that his recent allegations about how Boris behaved in these early months of managing the pandemic are mostly true (including his apparent comments about those over 80 not being so important) unfortunately the country was not listening as by then Boris was riding the Vaccine Bounce. The impressive vaccine programme delivered by our NHS – the very NHS that Boris has spent most of his political life trying to privatise and then belittles by offering them a measly 1% pay rise! While all his mates reap the benefits of relaxations on procurement to turn a big profit on consultancies and producing masks and PPE that don't come up to standard.

As well as having faith in the various Public Health personalities flanking Boris at the daily press conferences, looking back I have been ever grateful that I live in Wales where we have a sensible First Minister who looks at the evidence, engages with the people, businesses and services affected and then responds. Mark Drakeford has been doing a brilliant job in Wales, managing the health crisis as has our Health Minister Vaughan Gething. I know them both personally and the benefits of living in a small country through this pandemic have been enormous. I've felt that the Welsh Government have had my back – they've been on my side throughout.

The first lockdown here from late March until early July went by relatively smoothly for me. The sun was shining, I had loads to get on with in the garden and my allotment and I had some work to occupy me. My adult children all kept (and still have) their jobs.

We adopted a dog – a 9 month old collie, "Bob", who we love to bits.

Two of my children and all of my grandchildren live locally so we went through it all together. Sometimes we had to meet outside in difficult circumstances but we managed. There was also a sense in those early days that the pandemic would all be over in a few months and we could soon resume normal life again.

When the first lockdown was lifted in July – numbers of infections initially stayed low. We had a great summer. The sun shone and we got away to Cornwall and saw our best friends who now live in Devon – we re-charged our batteries in all sorts of ways. We can do this we thought!

Then of course we were back into lockdown by November here in Wales. It wasn't over by any stretch! We got through until Christmas as things heated up again. We managed to have all the family together for some festivities. Looking back on it all I can see that our holiday in Cornwall last September and the fact that we pulled off a Christmas family gathering at the end of 2020 kept me going for some time.

Then, I recall - it all went downhill. We continued in lockdown through January 2021 until April. That was a hard few months. It was winter, it was cold, the virus rates were high, and lots of people were dying. It was all a bit scary – you mean it's here to stay? And depressing. My husband's health was not great as he awaited a heart op, my daughter who works as a teacher in a secondary school was struggling, a close friend died under tragic circumstances, not of Covid but undoubtedly his health was impacted hugely (economically and socially) by Covid.

My daughter was working in a high risk environment and was understandably worried about infecting her aged parents; my son had a new born baby that had to be hidden away from family and friends; my other two sons were living a way away and we couldn't see any of them very much unless we were freezing around a camp fire under a gazebo we had hastily erected in our back garden! I had had enough of bloody Zoom meetings and retreated from work eventually taking the big decision to retire once my existing commitments had been delivered. It was all pretty grim for a few months.

We had weekly Zoom meetings with all the kids which helped and of course we felt privileged to live in a nice house with a nice garden in a lovely area by the sea. We had lovely walks nearby and had lots of opportunities to wonder at the beauty of nature. We were and still are, very lucky.

My husband had his big op in June 2021 which involved more self-isolation as everyone else was beginning to emerge from behind their shutters. I was not allowed to visit him in hospital which was very tough for us both but the NHS team who looked after him were amazing- the op was a success and he continues to make a good recovery.

In the last month it feels like we have got back to a more 'normal' way of life. We have recently attended a favourite music festival (a delight) and have a trip to Ireland to see close relatives planned for next month. We have made a number of visits in recent weeks to the beautiful coasts of west Wales to stay in a friend's caravan and all the family managed to get together again for a summer weekend at the family home. One is grateful for these small but important punctuations that certainly keep me optimistic and feeling very grateful for what I have.

What next? I'm not looking too far ahead. I don't know what I'll be doing in a few months' time. Like others I suspect I'm reluctant to make too many plans - I have enough EasyJet, British Rail and Brittany Ferry vouchers left over from cancelled trips to see me through, I don't want to gather up any more.

I expect more lockdowns and more jabs in my arm. I have my Covid passport and I still feel lucky but I am dreading another winter like the last one and I plan to do all I can to avoid it!

Not sure how but I'm working on it.

Shelley

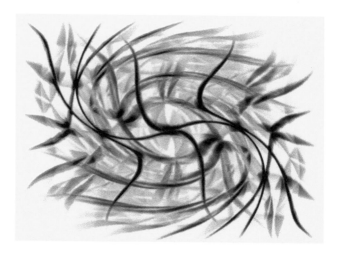

I keep thinking this nightmare will be over soon, but no it keeps rolling. I am feeling increasingly isolated amongst all my friends, all have had the jab and are now saying things along the line of "so and so has got covid, thank god they had double jabs or they could be so much worse!"

My daughter has been poorly with the virus, exactly the same symptoms as flu, and I was made to feel like a bad mother for not encouraging her to get the jab!

Where is this going to end!

It's been a strange 2 years! My husband's business went mental initially when 1st lockdown happened; we were caught so unawares with it! He has been in the disinfection business all his life but someone told him not to bite the hand that feeds you when he dared to speak out.

In some ways the lockdowns have been good for us as a family, as we still have our son and daughter at home with us, so we had some very beautiful family time, and it made us all slow down and take stock, love the small things in life all over again.

I am feeling sad as I write this, I'm frightened for the future and future generations.

I know there are lots of us out there that have the same views but the powers above keep bulldozing on, and I can't see an end to it. All I do know is me and my immediate family will not take the jab, so where that leads us all is anyone's guess at the moment.

Michelle - Our Lockdown Labrador

Our Lockdown Labrador is loved beyond measure,
We searched far and wide to find this absolute treasure.
He's a northern lad with a big job to do,
An assistance dog he'll be, and he's still only two!

Family life changed forever three years ago,
Our daughter aged 16, symptoms started to show.
Tic and Tourettes syndrome, took a whole year to assess,
So many tics causing lots of distress.

Our Lab is a gem, he'll give the help that she needs,
To walk out in public, overcoming her stress, as he leads.

Her to feel safe and secure, no longer ashamed,
Of the compulsion to twitch - she is not to be blamed!

He will lie next to her when she drops to the ground,
To add calm in a tic attack, he will be found.
Opening doors to alert - it's the right thing to do,
He's a dab hand at that, our golden dog Boo!

He's a whirlwind of fun, a super-strong boy,
Smart and devoted - a bundle of joy.
A light red fox Dudley, his eye colour rare,
Gentle and caring, our beautiful Boo Bear!

For my beautiful Maya Ann xx

Hayley

For me the last 18 months have been a mix of emotions.

At the start when we first heard of Covid in China and people dropping down dead in the street I didn't think it would get that bad and affect the whole world or the UK much if at all. We'd had bird flu, mad cow disease and maybe some others in my life time and they hadn't killed that many people, not in the UK or around the whole world that I can remember.

I started contacting friends around the world to ask how it was for them where they were. I had a friend still in China from when I lived there, and a few friends in Taiwan so I was interested to hear from them their perspective; as well as a guy in Singapore where they seemed, like Taiwan, to be doing well at responding and taking measures with low deaths. Other friends in Italy, The Philippines, Sweden, Australia, Portugal, Morocco and America also spoke about how things were and what was being done there. Maybe the UK wasn't doing enough? Boris seemed slow and useless, but I still didn't fear Covid or feel worried I was in danger or that it would get that bad.

I spoke with one friend in Singapore where they seemed to be taking the pandemic more seriously than in the UK; hotels and sports stadiums were being used as pop up hospitals and quarantining spaces so anyone sick was kept there and away from passing on the virus to others.

This seemed a good idea to me, that it might stop the spread, and it was making use of large spaces to help those who were sick when hospitals could get overrun. My friend in Singapore thought the UK were slow to react and weren't doing enough much like other parts of Europe and America.

In Taiwan they closed borders off to China very early on to stop it getting bad for them, they wore masks and took things seriously but from seeing my friends posts they didn't completely lock down and they could still do things and businesses didn't seem to take such a hit as ours here in the UK.

Every year the newspapers say our NHS is overworked especially in winter and it seems the government aren't looking after it or the staff. The Nightingale hospitals were made which sounded a good idea to help relieve the hospitals but then were never used.

My American friend in Shenzhen; Guangdong; China which has only the province Hunan between where she is and the province of Hubei where Wuhan is located told me on the 20th Feb 2020 that restaurants were back open to 50% capacity but with lots of rules. She was allowed to go out for walks, there were temperature checks everywhere you go, masks worn in all public places and the rule of being 1m away from others. Schools were closed with online teaching but opened back up around 18th March where masks had to be worn up until the end of June 2020. She said it felt like a zombie apocalypse and surreal but having been like it for 6 weeks people were getting used to it.

In Sweden my friend said masks were optional, most didn't wear them, businesses were open, some just reduced capacity, life seemed pretty normal. In Perth where my British friend is living life hasn't really been affected there much compared to other areas of Australia like Melbourne and Sydney. They have sometimes had to wear a mask outside for a week or 2 because of 1 case, and businesses are having the QR code check which many are complying with.

I read the daily cases and deaths online regularly for a few months to see what was happening, comparing the UK to other countries, reading news articles and watching the news updates but still not too worried. I thought I'd be off work for a couple weeks, a month at most and then back to normal.

I was also reading and watching videos that friends sent me that showed a different perspective to what was being shown to us. I'm pretty open minded and didn't dismiss anything, I looked into claims and researched what I was seeing and hearing that was different to the mainstream narrative. I luckily knew a number of open and like-minded people who also didn't believe all that the media and doctors on tv were telling us; it felt good to have others to discuss it with.

In April 2020 I started working in a supermarket where I was starting work at 4am to pick shopping that was being delivered to customers, this department dramatically increased due to more people not wanting to go out or be around others. We had a one way system in the store and the number of people in the store at any time was limited, though it still seemed 'too busy'.

From the end of July 2020 they started telling us we should wear a mask which I did at first but then finding it hard to breathe and realising it wasn't a law or compulsory I stopped, a few months later it seemed to be compulsory. I struggled with this but the management were pushing it and reminding us to put masks on as well as the constant announcements between every song on the store radio; it was draining and there was no break from the bombardment of fear and propaganda. I resented the masks, the struggling to breath, the uncomfortableness of it, the severe acne it gave me, it caused me jaw pain as well as it made my jaw lock and not fully open which my dentist confirmed was a condition called TMJ. I had had no issues with this condition before wearing the mask for 6-8 hours or more a day.

The tables in the canteen were rearranged with only 2 chairs allowed per table so that people could not sit next to each other, then in 2021 it became 1 person per table. When the rules changed and people from different households could meet in restaurants and bars they still kept the limited seating at tables.

I've not heard of any staff dying from Covid, but I've heard of a number who have had reactions and health issues since the jab and on two occasions when I've been driving to work someone has been trying to jump off the bridge that goes over the road to my supermarket and a third time I drove past someone who had already jumped.

Luckily I've had no pressure or communication to take the jab, and I won't be having it even if I am at risk of losing my job. In staff areas at the supermarket there is a lot of propaganda on posters about getting free Covid tests, washing hands, socially distancing and some on help for mental health too. I think the majority of my colleagues of all ages have had the jab, for a number of reasons. Some because they felt they should, some because they want to go on holiday, and some because they want life to return to normal.

Recently (mid-September) I asked one of our senior ex store managers about why the tables in the staff canteen are still for only one person when in cafes we can mingle and sit with others. He said its store policy from Head Office and they're just doing their bit as a duty of care to keep everyone safe.

I did question him saying we aren't standing 1 or 2 meters apart in the store and nor is anyone else so why do we have to do it in the staff room.

Customers can't see us and it's a shame we have to be spread out on break and not able to get together to relax and chat. If we want to do that we would have to go to the customer cafe in the store. This all seems very illogical to me - no sense to it at all!

My final comment to him was that there's no science saying it works and he said he'd pass on my views to Head Office. I'll let you know in Book 2 if he comes back to me with a comment from Head Office. I'm not holding my breath!

Months have gone by and I've spent so much time and energy looking into what has been happening and seeing things not stacking up.

I've been fortunate to have made so many new friends and find myself in a community of people who I would probably never have met had it not been for what has been happening.

Meeting all these people, people I can rely on, people who are on the same wavelength, who are critical thinkers and kind, caring and helpful, has been the best thing about the last 20 months.

Winter was hard last year at times, not having the community then that I have now. My life has changed so much and I am so grateful and happy that we are all there to support each other. Many of us have struggled with disagreements and fallouts with family and friends who think we have all lost the plot and are talking rubbish.

For me, family not being on my wavelength and not even listening to me to give me a chance to speak has been tough, especially close family members; I try to not let it bother me but it does at times. I try to just not speak about it or think too much about it, instead immersing myself in my new circle of friends and my new social life which has improved so much in the last 5 months.

I cherish and enjoy my new friendships and long for us to create a better, happier, freer, and less censored world for us all.

Jill

London turned into a ghost town when we went into the first lockdown with eerily empty streets and roads.

This emptiness highlighted the number of key workers vital to keep a big city running.

I would like to pay tribute to all of them - the street cleaners, refuse collectors, postal workers, transport workers and all the staff in food and pharmacy, not forgetting the often invisible people working in manufacturing and distribution to keep us supplied with essentials.

Many of us were able to stay safe at home but there were a significant number who went out every day to make sure that we had everything we needed.

My second realisation was how precious time is. For the middle-aged "losing" time may not be so crucial but for the young, whether at school, university or starting in jobs, they have missed vital time for education and development.

Those at the end of their lives have also been deprived of time with their loved ones and opportunities to be active.

I think particularly of my dear friend Brooks who just missed his 100th birthday and left us without the chance to say goodbye.

I shall treasure happy memories of his enchanting smile and boundless curiosity.

Kelly

PANDEMIC? I was living in Spain when the virus was first mentioned. I freaked out like a lot of people did, I was scared that I might die, as a smoker and single mother of an eleven year old the thought of a deadly highly infectious respiritory disease was terrifying. I was scared some of my family would die. My mind jumped all over the place with "what ifs". I had a major panic as I realised this deadly disease that was on the other side of the world yesterday, was now on our doorsteps.

We were given 2 days to prepare. People started panic buying in the supermarkets just before lockdown - then everything levelled out - the supermarkets were never empty. My question is "why toilet rolls?"

I do not suffer from anxiety but I did become very nervous when I went out to do my weekly supermarket shopping. I can remember seeing my neighbour as I pulled out in my car and saying to her "I'm shaking".

The fact was, apart from our weekly supermarket shop, we weren't allowed out of our homes and the police presence was severe.

The weekly shopping trip was a nightmare - going into the supermarket there was hand sanitiser, then you put your sanitised hands into plastic disposable gloves - you were already wearing a mask. Supermarket staff were in place to speak harshly and loudly if you did anything wrong.

I got fiercely told off in the supermarket by the security lady for having a conversation with another person; we were not allowed to stop and talk.

I felt very cross at not being allowed to talk - it was like Franco days. The security lady said there were people standing outside waiting to come in as the number of people allowed in the shop was limited. I did understand that but still felt angry deep inside at being told I was not allowed to have a conversation with another person.

Many of my lovely friends and clients did get stopped and never went shopping again, they got their husbands to shop as they felt so intimidated.

Let me explain being intimidated: the police would stand, often several of them, masked and with machine guns, on roundabouts and at road junctions. They would stop you and interrogate you "where have you come from and where were you going" you answered them and at times they would ask you to get out of your car to show them your shopping in the boot, to prove you had been shopping. If you had no shopping to show, you were in trouble. Very intimidating. Red Flag.

In the early days of lockdown I was sitting in my garden having a glass of wine, speaking to my friend down the road who was also sitting in her garden having a glass of wine; we decided it was ridiculous - she was 3 minutes away!

It was not logical that we could not sit on a terrace, albeit apart, and drink our wine together and so I drove down to her and sat in her garden, socially distancing and not touching anything.

Her mum was in her 90s and we wanted to be very careful not to put her health in any danger.

After a couple of weeks we were more relaxed.

Bearing in mind, we were both living without partners, for me, going from seeing up to 20 people a day in my work to being isolated at home, moments like these kept me sane and it was worth the risk.

After one of these secret wine drinking occasions, heading home, I saw the police on the roundabout ahead. Panic. My heart started racing - I had no shopping in my car. I was really scared. I felt like a criminal. Luckily they didn't stop me.

Later that evening I found myself thinking "I'm glad I got away with that" - next time I would definitely synchronise my secret wine drinking with my Mercadonna shop! Red Flag.

As a Hairdresser, we were initially kept on the essential list which made no sense at all. We all thought "Really - a close physical contact business like ours?" Red flag.

The rule was changed within 24 hrs and we stopped working. I couldn't work for 5 or 6 weeks, however, strangely hairdressers were amongst the first professions to be allowed to go back to work. Still didn't make much sense.

The only thing I could think of was that Pedro Sanchez had shares in the hairdressing industry!

I prepared to work in a different way, following the government guidelines. I could only have one client at a time with a 15 minute gap between clients to give me time to sanitise the whole area - chairs, my tools etc - before the next client. The bleach ruined my tools. I had to supply each client with a new sanitised gown and as I only had a limited amount of gowns in my salon I had to improvise. I came up with the idea of using bin liners, which I had to cut into shapes in a sanitised area, with sanitised scissors; I rolled them up and put them in individual bags to give each client as they arrived. Time and expense at the end of each day.

After a short time I really thought "I'm done with this - I really can't see the point in it." Red Flag.

Two weeks after returning to work, connecting with my clients; still at that point, none of us personally knew anyone, nor did we know of anyone who knew anyone who had contracted covid, ended up in hospital or died. This definitely didn't feel like the deadly disease we'd been told about.

I started relaxing - my fear was over.

I carried on with all the procedure with clients who were worried but most clients were not worried and wanted to carry on as normal, have their hair done and have a good chat, after all I was one of the few people, if not the only person, they had personal contact with.

Clients generally walked in with a mask around their chin and they would say "do I have to wear this" and I would say "not with me you don't". Discussions about the value of wearing masks started. Questions about everything that was going on started.

One of the popular conversations was how people were not dropping dead in the streets as advertised on TV.

At the end of the day, I did whatever made each client happy, respected each individual and their wishes.

I think it was about 3 or 4 weeks in I just decided not to be scared, I would discuss the numbers of deaths and all the information with my friends and sometimes with a brandy. At this point it was "Game Over" for me. Too many Red Flags.

Because of the restrictions I found myself, for the first time in my life, enjoying my clients and chatting with them without rushing to the next client. I had enough time to go to the loo, have a cup of coffee and something to eat during the day and when I finished work I felt relaxed.

Note to Self: "don't do as much in a day as you used to and you'll feel better for it"

At the end of the month I was earning less but feeling better healthwise. Should have been my wake up call but it wasn't.

When restrictions were lifted I immediately went back to my normal pace! I worked from mid/end June through to the end of July and then prepared to leave Spain at the end of August.

My son's school closed at the beginning of lockdown and as I had already taken the decision to leave Spain and return to the UK we didn't take the home education too seriously. I was under a lot of pressure preparing a large villa, single handedly for sale.

Home Ed - Really!

As the restrictions lifted in June the schools did not re-open as in Spain they break-up for the summer holidays by mid-June, and so they prepared to re-open in September with all children over 6 years old wearing masks.

Since then, I have heard stories from parents of how the children swapped their masks in the playground to have fun! Rather makes a mockery of wearing masks to protect them from a highly infectious disease!

I can't think of a lightbulb moment but I could see a divide, some were going along with the rules because they were nervous, some just because they felt they had to. In Spain you really felt you had to do what you were told

You could start recognizing the people who didn't believe what they were asked to do, who didn't think any of it was making any sense.

Meanwhile there were vicious conversations on social media with people snitching on neighbours and others for walking in the street when they weren´t supposed to - this was really horrible to see.

I left Spain on 26 August

I am fortunate as I still don´t know anyone who has died of covid and I still don´t know anyone who knows anyone who has died of covid.

I think everything was taken way out of proportion from the very beginning. All the "dropping dead on the streets" scenes we were told were coming to a cinema near us soon - did not happen. The forecast of deaths did not happen. We only heard about covid, no other diseases or deaths.

The biggest thing I do not understand is why the UK Government website stated clearly on 19 March 2020 that the virus is no longer a highly infectious deadly disease and then locked down the country on the 23rd.

I see madness all around.

My family think I am the mad one!

I have times when I wobble - nano-seconds - when I just think shall I do what others are doing - it would be much simpler. Trouble is I just don´t believe it.

Moving back to the UK, with a teenage son who was born in Spain, was always going to be challenging after 17 years. Covid made it harder as we were unable to launch our new lives, house searching, business, school, re-connecting with friends - doing all of this with the restrictions was a non-event.

I live in a village in Somerset with my family all around which was the main reason for returning to live in the UK, and if it hadn´t been for the love and support of my family things would have been very different. I had no help from Spain having left, and no help in the UK having just arrived.

Unfortunately, although fit and able to work I couldn't embark on a new business due to the 2nd lockdown.

I have now bought a house and found that, although everyone who is not working in an office is working from home, everything has gone slowly because of covid. It is the excuse for everything.

It is not that a covid virus did not/does not exist, but in my opinion it was taken out of all proportion and most government guidelines and advice made no sense at all. Lockdowns were based on number of cases - cases were based on tests - tests were not accurate. Common sense and logic tells me that does not add up!

People have died over the past 18 months and every death is sad but we have only heard of covid deaths and many of those were "with covid" not "from covid".

This autumn/winter will be interesting!

Alasdair & Lydia Walker-Cox

My husband, Alasdair, & I have been married for 31 years. We have been blessed with 7 wonderful children, the oldest now being 24 and the youngest 12. Our children have never been to school, they have all been/are being educated at home.

My Dad & I started a business 30 years ago in our local town centre of Droitwich Spa in Worcestershire. The shop sells cards, gifts, partyware & sugarcraft products. Dad had to retire 6 years ago to become a full time carer for Mum who was diagnosed with Alzheimers. My husband, Alasdair, then took over the running of the business from Dad and we employ family & friends to run it with him.

So this was the context of our lives when March 2020 hit and everybody's lives changed forever in one way or another.

My first memories of the lead-up to March 2020 were of weird and disturbing pictures being broadcast of people keeling over and dying on streets in China. Also of the way the Chinese authorities were dealing with the population to get them to keep themselves locked away.

Then came talk in our own media about over 70's and the vulnerable shielding themselves from this deadly virus. All extremely frightening stuff!

Then the bombshell came sometime towards the end of March when we were told that everyone would have to lockdown for '3 weeks to flatten the curve'. We dutifully closed our business & followed government guidelines as we were considered to be 'non essential'. The 3 weeks became 12 weeks and businesses like ours were bribed by grants & payouts to stay closed. It's worth saying here that many people who had only recently started up in business, or who were dependent on other businesses for their income, who now had to close, found themselves losing their livelihoods.

Our daughter & husband had their first baby on March 11th 2020. We saw our precious little grandaughter for the first 2 weeks of her life, then lockdown was announced and we were told not to have contact with anyone outside our own households. So for the month of April we had the agony of not being able to help or be part of this time in our daughter's life. Also my Dad was really struggling in his care of Mum with having no help from family members.

Towards the end of April I was starting to have doubts about the way in which the pandemic was being managed. A recovery rate of 99.7% was the figure for those not in the very old/very vulnerable bracket. I was seeing and hearing about the very harmful effects of lockdowns on the mental health of people who were scared, lonely and/or had lost jobs and social lives. I could see at this time that my Dad needed more help or he would be tipped 'over the edge' with looking after Mum 24/7. So from the beginning of May I insisted that we acted normally & helped him out by having Mum or being with her while he had some free time. Also, our daughter & husband had reached the point, from the data that was coming in, that the healthy young were really not affected by this virus. So we had no fear for the safety of our grandaughter & began seeing the family and helping out as would normally happen within a close-knit family.

So, at the beginning of July we re-opened our business with all the 'safety measures' in place. But all the while there were rumours that more Lockdowns would follow.

It came as no surprise, then, that at the end of October the 2nd lockdown was announced & it began on 5th November. We were also pretty sure there would be another one at the start of 2021 to co-incide with the vaccine rollout. We did our calculations, taking into account that we had thousands of pounds worth of Christmas stock to sell, and the government weren't offering us enough to cover our rent. In the light of these financial considerations, and because we felt it to be unfair to allow the bigger stores & garden centres to remain open whilst we had to close, we decided to stay open. We felt that we were no more of a health risk to the general public than Wilko's, B&M, Home Bargains, supermarkets, WH Smith's etc. Nobody was coerced to come into our shop, people did so at their own free will. Also we know of no one who was harmed by using the shop.

Since making this decision we have had multiple visits from the police and the council trying to bully us into closing. We have had Prohibition Notices & fines, multiple emails & letters. We continued to stay open throughout all of this harassment which covered lockdowns 2&3. The government bases it's decision-making for these lockdowns on rises in 'cases'. A high percentage of these 'cases' are from false positive test results. So with mass testing of healthy people and a huge number of 'cases' that aren't even ill people, the government can keep this whole narrative going.

On 17th August we were brought to trial by Wychavon District Council over our refusal to close. We lost and were told we would have to pay £44,000 in fines. I suppose we're still in some measure of shock at the enormity of the fines imposed. We shouldn't be, though, as what we find ourselves involved in has nothing to do with health, but has everything to do with politics.

We have appealed, so the story continues....

Lani Wisniewska

Hello Beautiful Souls.

I shall jump straight into it....
As I look back over it all, there is no room for any emotion to live within me; except from a well of gratitude bellowing with love and a passion I could now burn down whole cities with.

If I had to "label" lockdown I would say that the silence it has brought to me is a true gift that lead me to the compass of my heart. An epitome that froze our time. A sort of magik that gave us many moons to feel what lies beneath our sunken chests and many births of sunsets for us to digest.
   The conclusion I realise is that it doesn't take our eyes or thoughts to be able to feel the vibration of truth. In the midst of being frozen, I've allowed myself to "see" the light from the

perpetuating darkness flowing through. I've had time given to me. The world stopped and there was nothing distracting left to stop me from seeing what was real about me and about others.

Although most importantly, what was real about life altogether. No other remedy except silence can let us feel and see what's real about us. The illusion of eyes or even words are not something we need when it comes to getting to know oneself. I've seen so much from what lied dormant within me and I suddenly grew so much wiser from the process of silence.

As a true lover of writing, story telling, reading and anything books, I am the personality who takes a long time reading them. Not because I don't enjoy the writers words but because I like to pause on the sentences that vibrate with me. I desire to feel the essence of them more deep than I imagine spelling could ever go. It's not unlike music. The way it brings me to my senses or to my knees whilst my voice is in harmony. I'm such a deep soul and a sensitive person and like all of us I recognise music and it's intrinsic vibrations and the memories and recollections we gain from its melody are so intense from relation we could almost relive that moment the melody notes us back too. Lyrics and melodies are such a deep and meaningful translation to raise to a new life when certain moments in time no longer resonate when unfolding that next chapter of our uniquely, magnificent book of life.

I adore asking myself questions such as...
   What does that moment I'm feeling mean for me?
   Why does it feel this way?
   How could I cherish this moment from this feeling within me?
   How could I express myself within using this feeling in my future?
   Does it serve me to keep or doesn't it?

However I am here to share with you my story, and a piece of what I lived through during lockdown. A lesson in life that awakened my soul. Two castle moments in my life defused me during the most isolated hours that I have ever existed in. The ever so long days and nights with nobody to hold and care for me. I embody a deep knowing that being cared for in this life isn't always a given but it would have been nice. On the contrary when I say "castle moments" I mean to express that lightening had struck in a way that the imanginary castle that I created within my mind didn't have enough solid foundations for my soul to stay alive in.

Through those castle doors that felt so safe and warming, yet had no decoration inside and no people I could trust, tells a story of much hope but little loyalty and little love. As high and mighty as that castle felt it didn't embody anything of the truth at all but more of a glaze of protection with a thin ice that's about to explode underneath. It was just a matter of time before I surrendered to lay with the roots of rock bottom, letting them coat me and take me down under to see why I allowed myself the creation of this castle to begin with. The castle was a minute facit of who I truly was and who I was going to be.

The only part that I needed to take with me, whilst the rest crumbled, was the shame of my inner child and how I could hold hands with those fragmented pieces of self, that loyally remained with me and never left me bare, but gave me a sense of self to remember.

I am Lani by the way, I apologise for introducing myself so late. It's usually a trait of mine to go deep into something without introducing myself, so I guess I have my reasons.

I aspire to be an author of an eleven sequel children's healing collection and a book in process of a spiritual adventure of numbers. I'm a mother, a daughter, a sister, a newly god mother and a best friend. I dream of one day opening up my own Children's Healing Centre. I am a woman who has experienced much loss in my life and also a fallen victim of societal pressures. I come from a long line of ancestral karma that forged me and my hardened heart until the day I fell down into the world of silence and of what felt like nothingness.

The sudden eclipse and acceptance of the dark night of my soul, was actually what many call a spiritual awakening. I was faced with the reflection of my soul that I didn't understand, it didn't feel one bit like the reflection I saw in the mirror. I saw shame, ugliness, poverty and a nobody with nothing to offer anyone. That couldn't of been the soul that the universe was showing me, that unconditional love and bliss was far too tender for me; even though I always had a deep rooted feeling that I innately knew I could become so much more than what my world so far presented me with. Either way I didn't feel like I had a choice, the tenderness just kept coming to trigger me to promise to turn me inside out so I could finally feel again what darkness lied dormant underneath my surface. Layer after layer was presented to me until I finally felt empty and stripped of my castle. That is where I felt balanced when I was at a standstill in emptiness. It was all an illusion some might say, but if so it was an illusion that showed me the bitter side of life yet also a promise of the feelings of love I did desperately want but sadly with no foundation to it.

What a strange combination of triggers that spoke to my soul to awaken what was sleeping within me.

A purpose so that I could realise what it is I really wanted, so that I could know who I was. In order to know who we are we must understand who we are not. To be enlightened by that is to experience what it is we are not by having something we think we want. I used to take advantage of sweet yet now I recognise what sweet really is because I experienced bitter. I'll never take advantage of sweet again.

I now know why I was born here and I was given that time during lockdown to realise and accept my experiences in life so far. I

forgive myself for what I know now but didn't know then and I'm pretty sure
I'll say this again the next time. As a woman who has experienced much loss, wrestled with brokenheartedness and lived in grief from a falsity whilst having a soul of many lifetimes trapped inside a cage tightly locked by my inner child, it all became too much to bear.

The universe heard my prayers and called judgement upon me in the most isolated time. Lockdown.

Endings and death always come for man and all we can do is take death's hand and smile back with faith that the old chapter has already served us as far as it can go.

I'll forgive myself next time death comes for me again with more new knowing I can stand under and more death I can stand over. I'll rise quicker no matter how deep I let myself fall.

My castle shall have structure and beauty and secret doorways, mystery and pleasure, dignity and authenticty, love, light and a free flow of emotion and anyone who needs love is invited in this safe place.

I'm a perfect candidate to understand near death experiences, lonliness, no sense of self and a mirror to brokenheartedness.

Love is all around us and the power to speak more is to resonate and to resonate is to have support and support helps aid in our understanding of healing.

They say that the purpose of life is to find your gift and then give it away. I am proud to say that what I have spoken about today is my gift and I give it away in writing and the way I love others deeply. The point is I will always feel my gift within me. I will always have a vibration of unworthiness and loneliness tower over me when I desire to illuminate the world in my own way.
I often struggle to pick myself up during alone times, I often sit there in that pain of just knowing and when I do feel that scar I just can't move. My inner child freezes in time and tells me I'm

not good enough but I don't shrug it off; I fight through and I heal because I cry and let myself witness and feel that journey again so I can see what lead me here. Natural bodily healing is to cry. Feelings are a part of us. We don't just get rid of them, we keep them in a safe place in the memory pocket section of our brains.

Memories help us journey and see why we won't give up. We never know when we might need the assistance of those chapters in our book again. I'm almost certain that we will. There are many people in this world to help.

Our unique and special chapters help us resonate with others whilst we entwine a precious story together; sitting at the same table, feeling a walk in similar shoes, expressing our losses and hurts in each of our own intrinsic ways.

This collide is priceless and from the pit of our stomachs life saving. Now how about that for a sacred gift. I own going through my hard times and in fact I love it; a love so deep and unconditional like that also helps heal collective conciousness.

Love is so beautiful.

You may be wondering why I am keeping my personal experiences so tight to my chest and why I hadn't told you precisely the activating events but I just want to say that that doesn't matter so much in life. It's always our deep rooted feelings and the way these people or activating events make us feel that heals us. So I may be protecting these people who I've loved and lost and I may be protecting my childhood story but just know that the way we feel is all that matters, the rest is just for us to know.

Sadly we cannot choose how death and change meet us but we can decide how we meet that end and that we are remembered as people who lived.

Skye Coelho

Greetings from Spain, sunny on the outside, somewhat darker on the inside…

The release of a lab created virus to create global chaos as part of the plan for the 'Great Reset' caught me off guard. I had been preparing for global meltdown on many levels for years and was no stranger to the dangerous power and games of Gran Pharma, the most powerful mafia on the planet.

My extremely unpleasant personal experiences of Prozac, 'the miracle drug' lead me to investigating the hidden agendas, fatal side effects and much more back in the 90s. I was under no illusion as to what they were capable of and what happens to many who publicly confront them.

Nevertheless, despite watching closely as the first stories from Wuhan were being released in mainstream media and aware that the Brexit farce was being used as the great distractor, I was busy with my own huge life changes and momentarily took my eye off the ball.

My youngest daughter and I had decided to return to the UK to start a new life in January 2020, a journey which included both fleeing an airport fire then dangerous floods in the UK - possibly warning signs of what was about to come!

Part of our new beginning included a month in the Middle East where my sister resided, sharing some family time and discussing our new path and options.

We landed in Dubai in February 2020 and things were already speeding up. Masks and hand sanitizer were becoming mandatory in most indoor areas long before Europe. It was a shock and a jolt, and I was instantly on edge observing what was happening, how things were escalating and yet my friends and family back in Europe thought my concerns were exaggerated. No, I was not frightened of the 'virus' but afraid of the repercussions of 'control strategies' being put in place. I knew this was the beginning of a very long journey on all levels.

Borders began to quietly close around us whilst most people remained oblivious and believing the official narrative. I sat in a five- star resort on a day trip, tourists laughing and taking selfies around me, whilst I began writing a survival list for the future, anticipating economic collapse, food shortages and much more.

My family thought I was crazy, but my intuition told me this was it, the premonitions of global chaos and change I'd been feeling for years were finally coming true. Actually, it was a relief to feel the beginning of the shift. I told everyone the virus would be the tool used for control and implementation of changes to freedom that under no other circumstances would the majority of the global population agree to in so called democratic countries but through the most powerful tool of control, 'fear', they would manipulate the masses into doing pretty much what they wanted. The world was hypnotized, and all remnants of critical thinking and logic seemed to disappear overnight.

My daughter and I became sick, paranoia reigned around us, as suddenly the common cold, the flu and pretty much every other disease seemed to have miraculously disappeared and only 'The Virus' existed!

We visited a doctor who warned us that my daughter's symptoms seemed to be those of the virus but reassured us that with plenty of warm drinks, high dose of vit D3, C and zinc the worst should pass.

However, she warned us there was about to be a lockdown and we should leave the country asap. She knew before it became official news.

And so it happened, almost overnight without warning, we had 24 hours to leave the country, on the last two seats on Turkish airlines before Turkey closed its borders (our airline tickets were via Istanbul). Still the expats were incapable of believing that Dubai would go into lockdown or that Emirates would stop flying. Cognitive dissonance? A complete inability to process the idea that their perception of reality was about to come crashing down? Surely things like this only happened on Netflix?

The chaos had truly begun: The airports were brimming with anxious passengers hurrying to return to their home countries. The stress was palpable.

We cried as we said our farewells to the family, already knowing things would never be the same again. Turns out I was right sadly; over the following nine months we would lose three of our dearest family members in tragic circumstances.

It was a hideously stressful and bizarre journey: We returned to a half empty Gatwick airport, very eerie indeed. As we sat in the airport hotel attempting to process the enormity of what was going on, feeling lost and disoriented, things suddenly became much worse. The person we were meant to be living with suddenly decided we were no longer welcome (all our belongings were there at his property).

Our UK family were trapped in different parts of the world, their flights cancelled and unable to return. Having lived away for many years, we were very disconnected from old friends and suddenly it dawned on us we had nowhere to go. We sat in the hotel for four days frightened and exhausted, our savings rapidly depleting.

The first news was that Spain had closed its borders but then a glimmer of hope appeared when we found out that nationals and residents were being allowed back in. So much for our new life back in the UK.

Our return flight to Spain was the strangest experience ever, ten of us passengers on a BA flight, all in masks and silent. Even the cloud formations looked completely different, perhaps due to a reduction in air pollution? Our return was not a happy one, indeed it was extremely traumatic.

My frightened father picked us up and almost threw us out of the car when we arrived home. I was darkly amused at his appearance, wearing marigold gloves and a huge scarf covering his nose instead of a mask, he had the appearance of a deranged terrorist...

That was the last glimpse I would have of him for a long while as we entered one of the strictest lockdowns in the world aside from Italy and Wuhan. It was mental hell. Myself, my two daughters and four cats locked in a flat for months apart from occasional supermarket and pharmacy trips, no exercise allowed. Constant police patrols and even the military at one point were sent in to intimidate. I felt I was living an Orwellian nightmare and my daughters feared for my sanity.

I spent most of those days researching to the extreme, everything from CIA files, Wikileaks, government files, pharmaceutical sites, tracked down whistleblowers, looked at Climate change stories, Solar cycles, UN agenda 2030...the list is endless. I saw the beginning of censorship in ways I'd never seen in the West before. I refused to go out on the balcony and applaud the health service telling my kids I felt I was part of the Fourth Reich…

I discovered people on YouTube agreeing with me even if most around me still thought I was overreacting…

From the moment we were told we would be 'quarantined' for only two weeks I knew it was bullshit and lies. On what planet does a real 'Pandemic' disappear in two weeks? Of course, they would not tell the truth at any point and still people believed their governments had their best interests at heart. I refused to believe the official narrative that cash was being declined because of the virus which was absolutely nonsensical when it was evidently the beginning of openly eradicating cash and ushering in the digital currency era and social credit system. Slowly people around me began questioning.

From day one the numbers did not add up. I continued with my prolific research which resulted in my book, '2020 when time stood still' a story which I described as a 'Sci Fi/fantasy/thriller in order to sugar coat my damning discoveries and accusations of government-controlled genocide.

Tragically In August 2020 my young cousin was murdered alongside his partner in Malta. We attended his funeral in the UK and attempted once more to start afresh there only to be plunged back into another lockdown, losing my job and in December returned back to Spain yet again wondering what the hell was going to happen next.

My friends and acquaintances really began 'waking up' which was a big relief in some very lonely moments. I became part of a dissident movement and my friend and I organized protests locally and participated in a global protest in Spain's capital, Madrid where I connected with Chinese whistleblowers who confirmed my findings on Wuhan that went back long before the official stories.

These have since been confirmed or rather admitted by international governments. I would also end up speaking face to face online with some of the world- famous whistleblowers who I had seen interviewed at the very beginning of this unbelievable saga.

Sadly, my favorite uncle, my father's brother, suddenly died in Stockholm. His death was blamed on the virus though he had Lewy bodies dementia and other complications and six weeks later, my worst nightmare came true: my father became ill, a very fit young looking 78-year-old, who was less fearful than he had been in the beginning yet still refused to travel. Sadly, he never got to meet his new grandchild in Dubai through fear yet instead was diagnosed locally, alongside my mother who barely had a symptom, with the 'virus' as well as other complications and we were plunged into hell.

The horrors of which I'd read about; the dreaded ventilator, the rules barring us from being with our loved one etc. I only saw my father conscious one more time and Thank God, I told him then I loved him before he was put in an induced coma from which he never recovered.

We fought tooth and nail to be by his side. My sister travelled twice from Dubai fighting to see him, even though she had been vaccinated and had negative PCR tests they refused to allow her in, the only visit was to say goodbye when his heart and lungs could no longer withstand the ventilator. The pain is unbearable, being separated from a dying loved one. My anger at the unjust system, nonsensical rules and overwhelming grief at times is too much and as I write this, I feel I will never recover from this pain.

I long to tell my father my stories of the Chinese whistleblowers I met, how I appeared on their dissident news channel with over 160,000 views, he would laugh but not be surprised. One of the last things he called me was his wild child. Losing my father during these dark times has been the worst experience of my life.

From the very beginning one of my biggest concerns was for people's mental health which would be dangerously compromised through fear, isolation and loneliness. A very poignant image which will forever remain imprinted upon my mind was the scene of local children's parks/play areas closed up with police tape as if they were crime scenes. There was no sound of children's laughter and play. It was desolate. I knew then that children and young people were going to bear the brunt of horrific decisions taken by the authorities which would affect them for the rest of their lives, being told not to touch, hug or kiss their friends and

relatives. I have studied clinical hypnosis and know the effects of such fear tactics on a young impressionable mind.

I was correct, and as time went on suicide rates began to go sky high particularly amongst young people losing hope for the future. Tragically I personally know two cases very close to home.

For me the mass media is one of the biggest culprits with their sensationalist fear and blame tactics, they have behaved in an unforgivable manner. I pray one day, alongside governments, they will be put to trial.

I continue fighting for my daughters' futures and for the hope that despite this current darkness, there is light at the end of the tunnel for a better earth and a conscious awakening.

Every day brings new challenges; my saviours are quiet times in nature, friendship, music and my dark sense of humor.

In the meantime, who knows what will have happened from now till this book is published?

The mind boggles…

Pandemic words and phrases:

we can´t let up now save lives now **PPE** social distancing jabbathon

contactless delivery virologist

superspreader **variant**

furlough

support bubble covidiot

scamdemic

12 weeks to flatten the curve **stay alert** Hydroxychloroquine

unexpected shortfall maskne close contact

key workers **pandemic** the rona

non essential travel track & trace ivermectin CDC

clotshot **5G**

It´s been a long year **self-isolating** **quarantine** covexit

home schooling

2 metres **SARS-CoV-2** **PCR**

sacrifice Blursday

lockdown

working from home WFH

the R number

censorship NHS overwhelmed look into my eyes

firebreak **new normal** government guidelines

booster vaccines

hands, space, face **Moderna**

stay sane **eat out to help out**

zoom quiz

vaccine passports **Oxford AstraZeneca**

mRNA wash your hands vaccine confidence

conspiracy theory

promoting prevention

Netflix non essential retail green list **masks**

return to normal **save lives**

Wuhan stay home anti-vaxxers

Have they reassured you or driven you mad?

spike proteins **like no other**

tier system herd immunity

covid plan B   hand sanitisers   **green list**

long covid

test centre short illness   science update

unprecedented **Pfizer-BioNTech**

let´s keep going   one step closer

stay safe we´ll beat this

green list be cautious

covid stone protect the NHS   pop up clinics

essential workers couch to 5K

contact tracing **covideoparty** epidemiologist

facebook expert   uncertain times

vaccine rollout the roadmap

outdoor dining

panic shopping **transmition**

covid plan A   unsustainable

pull together protect others

lockdown lite   no jab no job   doomscrolling   rise in cases

Sue and Stuart, Brittany, West France

So many different thoughts, opinions, beliefs, each one different as we all are from each other. I am going to try and make this short and succinct, but as it is all going round in my mind .....

Just a short background on my husband, Stuart and I; we have now lived in France for 17 years, 8 of those in Brittany in a small hamlet of 6 houses, 5 mins away from a small town and also right in the countryside with fields and trees. The Nantes Brest canal is 5 mins walk on a path through woods and then onto the towpath. It is calm, quiet and exceedingly pretty. We have a fair sized garden and can also wander around the hamlet, which most of the time has just 7 inhabitants, so it is quiet and there is lots of space.

We are semi-retired, have an income and pension from the UK and my husband works within the French system doing repairs and renovations, so we do not have a job to go to and we are safe financially. Of course all that I have said makes it easy to realise that we did not have a lot to worry about with pressures from work, people, or city /town living, and for those reasons Covid did not impact us very much personally.

I should add that none of our immediate family were affected or ill even. Friends that had it recovered without problems, so for that reason we were even more fortunate, which brings me to the first point.

Just before it hit us here in France, we had a great sadness in the family. My sister's eldest son had been living in France for a year or more having escaped problems in the UK and was trying to sort himself out and find somewhere to live and work. He struck lucky and found both for a short few months, but was unsettled and with issues of poor mental health and subsequent disappointments he tragically took his own life here in another department 4 hours from us.

Stuart and I were first to find out and I had to phone my sister in the UK, and we also dealt with all the legal officialdom and funeral arrangements. With the younger son and wife coming over to take back his belongings, my sister came out 2 weeks later to collect his ashes.

It was a huge shock and great sadness but he had attempted suicide before on several occasions. Just after this, in the spring, Covid hit us all here.

Strict confinement (or lockdown in the UK) began with all its heavy restrictions. What I am going to say almost sounds wrong and cruel, but for us it meant quite simply we had a space to grieve properly here in our home and surroundings without any pressures on us personally. The one being that I couldn't get over to see my sister, but we of course talked and cried often and I knew that she and her son and my sisters partner were supporting her and each other.

In fact I learned from this that one could get through something like this from a distance. It was very hard and very sad not being able to be with my family, but it did not affect my grieving, and grieving was just what I could do here with no pressures to have to do anything else, see other people, go out, put on a brave face. Nature all around, the coming of spring, planting in the garden, hours and hours indulged in tears memories thoughts and great sadness. But the lockdown gave us the time to do it all and for that strange reason and our circumstances it was not difficult. Lockdown gave us space to grief properly, and fully in private.

Here in France we watched all the news, here and in the UK, and felt that on the whole the French government were clear, and gave regular precise and understood views and rules regularly. At the beginning we had to have an attestation or paper with 6 reasons as to when one could go out and the reasons why. Time date and signature were required and had to be carried with you.

We always felt that that was a good and clear way of checking your need and taking the responsibility. In fact we were and still are reasonably impressed at the beginning as to how everyone around us did follow guidelines in shops, and the local town, but it was very 'surreal'; I think is the word.

I was a nurse all my life and latterly worked in the UK as a palliative care nurse in a hospice.We had time and space and the facility and the skills to look after people at the end of life in a wonderful personal holistic intimate way, accommodating patient and family's wishes, to make the end of life as dignified and gentle and as peaceful for the patient and family. A wonderful privilege.

Above all a gentle safe loving supportive environment with great personal contact which brings me to a second point:

Often, I could not watch the suffering, the incompleteness of life. The lack of familiar loved ones, the intimacy that I have just described, when it just wasn't possible to begin with; the mask wearing, not being able to see the patients face, nor the doctors nor nurses faces nor expressions, cut me to the heart.

I would cry and cry and would have to switch off from the tragedy and awful abruptness of it all. The one thing I couldn't bear seeing was the patients being removed in their thousands so abruptly, to be taken to hospital and never to see their family again or return home.

But the fact that there was no visiting was so hard to bear!

For me, one of the most heartfelt comments by an ICU nurse was that she was being haunted by the impersonableness, and the distance, and lack of contact as a compassionate human being, who has been trained in the skill of providing all those elements. That comment really stopped me in my tracks.

Also the speed of admissions, the speed and rapidity of deaths, ie "the turnover". I continually wondered and was afraid for all the medical staff dealing with this day after day, month after month, and wondered how long they could continue and what terrible after effects it would have on all concerned. That took a lot of my thoughts and it hurt for those people being, all the time, so courageous and selfless. I think the last point is difficult.

It is just my opinion, Stuart's too, that we did find it very hard to understand those people who thought it was all a conspiracy.

Those people who found it hard to follow regulations and put everyone else at risk. We felt that it was selfish and couldn't really understand the thinking behind it. Surely they could see with their own eyes and listen, and be aware of the magnitude of a global pandemic, Yes, I know that the governments in most countries, all probably, did not get it right sometimes, or often, were not open and truthful and misled the nation, but not in our lifetime has anything been on such a huge scale.

Impossible to have and follow a blueprint of how it should be managed and the sheer relentless pressure of it on everyone on a daily basis!

What a responsibility!

I have been reading, more than ever in confinement here in France, and enjoying filling huge gaps in my knowledge of world history, particularly of ancient civilisations, and how archaeologists have still many questions about the sudden ends of past civilisations.

Plagues and diseases and natural catastrophes ended these worlds. The global catastrophes still are happening all around the world as we degrade and abuse this wonderful world of ours. But we, globally, will continue, as over the millennia, we have discovered amazing new and unknown technology to deal with events such as this.

The discovery of reliable and generally safe vaccination programmes as we have seen already have stopped other diseases from killing people and now in a miraculously short time scientists were able to with their skills work together and rapidly find a new vaccine to confront Covid 19. Personally we think that this is the only way forward, I am convinced that without it we would still have been losing the huge numbers of people that was happening until the programme started.

The last thing that I will always remember is that as inhabitants of this planet we have shown and demonstrated as: individuals, teams, nations, that there is a way of working together to overcome and manage these events!

There are amazing people everywhere, being amazing; helping each other, inspiring each other, coming together, not competing and being greedy (though that too is very evident everywhere) but the will to survive is great, and I feel the only way to do that is coming together; understanding, informing and being tolerant!

Our family has been so fortunate in so many ways through this event. What a time to go through! We just have to learn from it. It is an opportunity we cannot deny, or not learn from.

I am forever grateful and thankful and that in the end is all I can say!
And I see HOPE.

Nicola

The worst thing for me was the inability to see and hug my mother. She is extremely vulnerable, so extra precautions were needed. Before shielding was fashionable, she was already doing it, as she fractured her back and was unable to go out.

I didn't rush up to see her immediately as it's a 500 mile round trip; I was at work, then we had booked a trip abroad, so waited to visit her on Mothering Sunday - to make the day special for us both. Well that was the plan, I was devastated that lockdown happened that weekend! Lockdown progressed, as we all know, so I kept in touch with her by phone and FaceTime: at least that was something.

Time went on, and I stuck rigidly to the rules. I'm a teacher at a local primary school, I was working from home as I am considered to be clinically vulnerable myself. I went out for daily exercise and felt blessed to live by the sea, and further blessed by the amazing weather we had!

Work was hard - I felt guilty that I wasn't in school and that others were, so I went above and beyond to do as much work from home as I could - especially as my job share was signed off - to take the pressure off those at the chalk face. It seemed to work.

My mother's birthday, at the end of June, approached and Boris said that we could meet up with others from outside the household as long as we kept our distance and were outside. Hooray!.

At last I was able to plan my trip to stay with a sister, who lives near my mother. I was to have a separate floor in their house, so we could maintain social distancing.

A few days later I arrived in the north - unbeknown to my mother - and knocked on her door. Thankfully she has a strong heart, as she was absolutely amazed to see me. Of course she invited me in and wanted to hug me - I declined both, though it was hard, but at last we saw each other, it was truly wonderful!

We hadn't seen each other for over 7 months...

Graham

How carefree it seems we were before the curse of Covid struck. Travel, work, seeing family and friends with no expectation that the normal way of life for most of the planet's inhabitants was about to change.

An avalanche of news, opinions, conflicting advice and scientific guidance consumed by us all and leaving Governments of the world's diverse nations to try to decide what action to take against this unseen threat to protect their populations.

Should we ignore it, should we vaccinate, if available, or like Belarus choose a more bizarre course of action and instruct the people to drink more vodka and spend more time in the sauna!

Only one thing is certain, whatever action any Government takes, criticism will follow after the event.

All the while we waited for Covid to hit us it was like waiting for an invasion and hoping " it won't happen to us" and then the fateful day when lockdown became vital to stem the spread and each day the roads, towns, cities and skies fell silent ... like an eclipse without end.

In this country at least, we have had massive financial government support for the majority of the population but even with this help it is inevitable that many companies will not survive and jobs will be lost. Let us hope that those who have suffered most and lost family, friends, jobs and homes can rebuild their lives.

And now we are at a point when hopefully the worst is over, albeit with thousands of lives lost. But this is a threat we must learn to live with and combat as it mutates in future, with a daughter extremely unwell and isolating with covid, despite double vaccination, as I type this, I am very conscious of the fact that this is not a time to be complacent.

We must live our lives again as normally as possible but remaining aware that we need to change the way we treat the planet, it´s population and our food chain for the safety and benefit of ourselves and our future generations.

Here endeth the lesson.

Bill

I have listed a few key moments in my life over the past 18 months and divided them into "**A**" for agony and "**E**" for Ecstasy. Generally it is chronological.

E - The generosity and necessity of strangers volunteering and getting us food supplies in the first 2 weeks of lockdown, when supermarkets were overwhelmed. End March/Early April 2020.

A - Fear of death , as a diabetic, and the thought of never seeing my wife, my sons or my friends ever again.

E - The spiritual valve of my daily walks and writing.

A - The constant sanitising of all supermarket deliveries.

E - The immense relief of getting the first vaccination, coupled with the unbridled joy of everyone there, those getting jabbed and those jabbing, in equal measure.

A - The total absence of physical contact with family and friends for so long.

E - Finally hugging my boys again on July 11 2021. A deeply meaningful moment which I shall never forget.

Brenda

Interesting times.

As a psychic medium I believe everything has a reason and we have to trust this. I probably see things from a different angle.

The well respected medium Sylvia Brown wrote a book in 2012 where this exact virus was predicted, and she said it would disappear as quickly as it started.

When all this began, I said to my daughter that the biggest problem would be fear, and I feel that this is true. The mind rules the body so negativity and fear play a huge part in our physical health.

I live in a small Spanish village, barely affected, apart from following the basic rules, but life here has been very normal, I hardly ever wear a mask, and I have declined the vaccination, we kiss and hug, same as always.

I have no fear, our journey is planned before we come into each lifetime, with a soul contract, I cannot change the main things that will happen to me. The day I die is written in my contract.

I have upped my vitamins, I live a healthy lifestyle anyway, but it makes sense to boost your immune system.

I also believe that as we look back in history, from the black plague, Spanish flu, nature takes it upon herself to occasionally have a cull, whether because we are over-populated, or for whatever reason she feels is necessary.

The one positive thing I see is that most people have re-assessed their lives, realised what is important or what or who they need to clear from their lives.

My clients are mostly like-minded people, and although obviously illness and death are horrendous to deal with, most people feel they have learnt something from this time, hopefully that we all need to be kinder, more caring, tolerant and understanding.

Let's Hope.

Wesley

As a Funeral Director in London I saw in March 2020 there was an increase in deaths; makeshift mortuaries were set up around London in full view at crematoriums and coroners mortuaries, but never full. I know of one not in use.

Then work quietened down; many PCR positive deaths were then labelled as covid but it really was clutching at straws and makeshift mortuaries were all taken down by summer.

Suicides had gone through the roof, mainly young men all summer long, then the quietest autumn on record followed.

When vaccinations started in January 2021 the numbers went up, with no PCR positives coming through but influxes of deaths and new makeshift mortuaries, this time not in full view.

In June, having been doing this job for two years, I had the most amount of funerals to deal with in one go - 12 deaths aged between 40 and 60; no record of if they were vaxxed or not but that was the age group.

This summer (2021) has been very quiet.

Jan

My story so far.......................

My name is Janice; however, I am called Jan, JW, Skippa, Lady Jan, CieCie and Boss Lady, Plum Pie, Jancie and I answer to all as these names mean something to me and represents my home life, love life, work life, family life and friends. I live in Perth, Western Australia with my husband and baby girl Dulcie, an Italian Spinone.

When Covid kicked off in a big way in March 2020, we were all sent home from work to start a lockdown of which we had no comprehension or knowledge as we really do live a very free life here in WA.

Our governor of the WA state is very firm and fair and said that he treats all his population as his own family and as such has an enormous responsibility to make sure we were all safe and well and so he shut down everything to lock out Covid.

At first it was fun, working from home with no hour-long commute was very appealing and for the first day or so, PJ's and UGGS were the order of the day and the best bit – no bra!

By about day 3 or 4 I felt very undone, unkempt and each day started to feel as if it leaked into another – like being on holiday because you could dance to your own beat and do what you wanted even though we all were working, but the times got a little blurred. I found myself starting at 7.30am and not actually moving from my desk until 6 or 7 at night, with natural breaks of course, but way too much sitting and working on a computer getting more and more tired.

So, week 1 went by and then it was 3 weeks later and now we had settled into a much better routine, getting up and about and getting on with it! (As my mum would say!) Then disaster – I received a call from my family telling me that my mum had been rushed into hospital and was currently in ICU with heart and kidney failure and it was all very serious.

So, when you leave your family behind in UK you go knowing and understanding that this scenario may happen at any point in time – but you can always get on a plane and fly home and be with your loved ones in 24 hours as you fly backwards in time from Australia to UK.

However, with covid and the country shut down and the countries in between Australia and UK closed it was going to be a challenge to get back.

Hurdles to overcome: -
- Get back before anything worse happened to Mum.
- Get an exemption from WA government to fly out and leave Australia.
- Get permission from my workplace to travel.

- Get an exemption from the Australian government in Canberra to leave the country.
- Get letter from my mum's specialist in the Intensive Care unit to relay to the WA government that it was 'end of life' issue and imperative that I travel to be with her.
- Get all this processed and through in 3 days as the first plane out of Perth via Emirates Airways was on the Thursday night and this started on the Monday – I had to be on that plane.
- Challenge accepted – I GOT ON WITH IT! Heard that before remember!!
- Long story short, with the help of my family and friends and some professional advice I got on that plane and headed home.

What I did not expect was the journey home was surreal and very very different from any that I had experienced before, and I have travelled for 40 years round the globe.

At Perth airport we were met with doubled up security with new check in desks that needed all my paperwork allowing me to leave Australia – all good.

Next stage was to get my Australia passport unlocked – as I have dual citizenship, I had to travel using my Aussie passport which was blocked by the government – at this stage I realised that I was not in control of my freedom and it was a strange feeling, but something you must get over quickly when you need them more than they need you!

Once my passport was unlocked, I got my boarding pass and walked through to the air side – everything was closed. No tourists, no duty free, no hustle and bustle no nothing!

I usually sit in a very nice lounge have a meal and a gin and tonic and trot off to my lovely seat – an empty departure lounge with maybe 25 other people all distanced, all of us wearing masks – all of us a little bit anxious as we departed Perth.

Arrival in Dubai was also very weird. Anyone who has been through Dubai knows how busy that is – but as I walked through the arrival halls – no one was there, no beep beep of the taxi cars carrying our older family members – just me expecting a crowd of people to come through the doors – but silence – nothing was happening.

Again, no duty free, nothing there because most of it is out of China so that was a non-starter. No lounges to sit in – just a welcome Costa coffee which is always a lovely thing.

On the plane we had to wear masks for the 22 hours we were flying. The staff were brilliant in doing their absolute best to take care of us in extremely difficult circumstances. I slept the whole way, with my eye on the prize – Mum.

My brother was at Heathrow to pick me up and as I came through the arrival doors, he had held up his phone where he had mum on facetime so she could see me arrive and stop worrying!!! She gave me a smile that I will never forget that went straight to my heart and I knew I was where I needed to be. My brother dropped me off at my friends where I was to stay for 14 days in quarantine.

I had daily calls and Facetimes with Mum but she had tubes in and it was difficult but I asked her to never give up and she promised me that she would fight to get well and she never broke a promise!!!!

Day 15 my friend's son drove me to the hospital where my mum had recovered enough to be wheeled out to the garden with all her tubes etc and I sat 15 metres away across a car park as I was not allowed near her for medical reasons until I had had 2 more covid tests. We waved at each other, and I have never felt so helpless in my life. I wanted to run and hold her and make her better, but I could not and had to 'Get on with it!'

But my mission was accomplished – I made it home, she made it through the ICU and treatments and in another week, she came home to her house, and I moved in to spend a month with her, sorting out things that she wanted, helping my step dad with this enormous change and trauma that had happened.

With all that said, there are some really funny things that happened along the way. Here's a couple: -

1. The specialist that asked my mum how long she had lived in her house – reply: 25 years and previously 35 years locally – so why can't we find you in our records? Response: I don't willingly go into any buildings with crosses on the outside – the truth – before this event mum had not been back to a hospital since she had my brother in 1965!

2. A very old man in the next bed to mum in ICU all hooked up to machines was explaining to his wife where the cheque book was and what money was in what account if he did not make it through – after some time and clearly confused she replied that he really ought to ask the doctor what to do about his ingrowing toenail!

During this time away I could work remotely and did so every day until my mum was strong enough and got her confidence back as it was a shock for her to realise that even she could break! So, after a month I reluctantly left the UK headed back to Australia with a heavy heart to carry on with my life, job and dreams with my husband.

But before that, I landed in Perth and was driven by full blown blue flashing lights police brigade to a hotel where I had to remain in 1 room for 14 days, have numerous covid tests and pay approx. 1500.00 for that privilege – and that is how I see it – thank you for the Australian government to let me go home, thank you for allowing me back in – (not so easy now) – I did all that was asked of me and got the prize – seeing and holding my mum.

Many thousands of people have not been so lucky – they have lost their parents and friends and family during this terrible time, not been allowed to see them in their hours of need and they have in some cases passed alone.

So that leaves me with the question of what is happening now – a year later – Eastern Australia is in total lock down, Western Australia has zero cases of covid, we are doubly vaccinated, and we are all free to do whatever we want to within the confines of WA – England fits into WA 58 times approx.! But I can't fly home now to see my family and friends as our governor has stopped us moving around the world and potentially bringing covid back into WA.

So, what to do..............................

In my darkest hour, I had to trust and believe that the specialists in ICU gave the correct medical treatment to my mum – without it she would have died.

I therefore have the same trust in the medics now – I must have faith as I did before and so I wait, until we are free to travel and be in the arms of the ones I treasure.

Love
Janice, Jan, JW, Skippa, Lady Jan, CieCie and Boss Lady, Plum Pie, Jancie xxxx

Veronica

"The Things I Lost - there are a lot of things I could say about lockdowns, but today, I will simply focus on the things that I lost due to the long periods of shut-downs and restrictions that we had last year in Melbourne, Australia.

I was in my final year of High School, and in the end, I had 115 days of being at school, and 96 days of distance/online learning.

I missed months and months of school that I will never get back. Months of time with my friends, with my teachers, enjoying my final year of school - at school – all gone.

All those little moments with other people and classmates, getting to see and interact with others, being there at lunchtime and recess – all gone.

The extracurricular activities that I enjoyed? Gone.

After-school sport? Yep. Clubs? Yep. Orchestra? Yep. Gone. Half of the graduation activities that we should have had, that I'd been looking forward to for years?

All of that's over; I'll never get to do them, and it's a loss that I will feel for the rest of my life.

It didn't have to be this way.
It never should have been this way.

I will never, ever forgive those who put us through it".

Michael Flannagan

I doubt there's been anything in the last century that has impacted day-to-day living worldwide, more than COVID 19.

That effect will continue for generations to come because the virus will be with us for generations to come. Just as we continue to talk about The Black Death, The Plague. The Pestilence, The Great Mortality, we shall speak of COVID 19.

It's earned a place in history, and like the Black Death, suppositions of its origin will surround what will be written about our confrontation with the SARS virus.

Just as the bubonic plague caused other plagues, so shall it be with COVID. No amount of religious fervor, mysticism, or denial will erase what the world has experienced from this pandemic which is what inspired me to write this poem: The Voice Of COVID.

If I were to be honest I'd have to say I wrote the poem out of anger and frustration.

I have found three kinds of people concerning how we deal with COVID exist: those who have faith and confidence in science, those who genuinely have reservations, and those who simply don't care.

I am one of those who trust in science; ergo, I am vaccinated and would advise others to do so. I also know those who, for some reason, don't share the same trust in science as I do, and I respect their decisions because they follow guidelines: masks and social distance, etc. They are not willing to risk putting themselves and others in danger.

There is also the third, dangerous group that sees no need to protect themselves, their loved ones, or the general population, and those are the ones that infuriate me to the core of my being. How anyone, during a worldwide pandemic, would feel it is their right to enter a plane, a hospital, a school as if there is no pandemic is beyond my understanding of fundamental concern for society.

Anti-maskers, anti-vaxxers attack in the name of "their freedom".

Sadly, the pandemic has become an object of political polarization where politicians are more concerned about power and politics than people, but here we are. COVID has been a two-edged sword.

Not only has it reminded us of what matters in life, but it has also revealed the depth of human cruelty. It has shown us that we need to work to improve society and allow compassion for others to take precedence.

If humankind refuses this basic challenge, something smaller, but more lethal, is at our doorsteps.

The Voice Of COVID

I'm not much, just a small thing.
Can't be seen by light microscopy,
Nucleic acid dressed in a protein coat
So invisible. You'd think I don't exist
But I do.
Can't say I am super intelligent
Can't even survive on my on
I seek the living cells of unsuspecting hosts:
Those who rely on the strength of invincibility
Those who walk in a world of no concern for me
I'm everywhere, like your devotion, like your opposition
I don't desire castles, riches, or your permission

I am the master of my fate—and yours if you let me
I seek a home in your lungs by way of your parties
Your feasts, churches where faith is supposed to protect
I hover in the air amid your sad funerals, forever seeking
Since you ignore my nature, you leave me no choice
I will rob you of your future, cut your dreams short
Mothers, fathers, sons, daughters, friends, and foes
Are mere words without meaning to me-I seek flesh
Diseased or healthy-I don't care-only living tissue
Without the warmth of your body, I am nothing
I need you to create mountain of detritus.

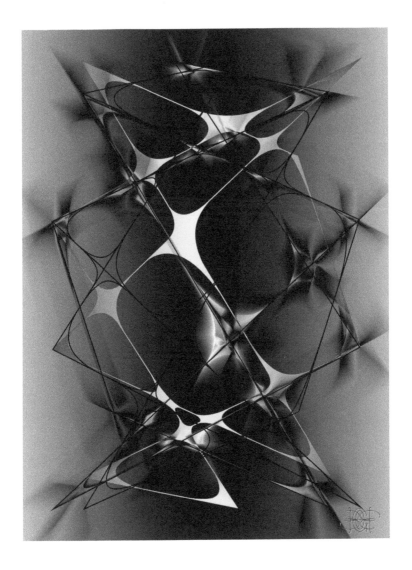

Sometimes I think the human race
is blinkered!
We are but a grain of sand on an
infinite beach of literally
immeasurable size.
We are like a single cell organism,
or molecule, amongst millions,
living inside a grain of sand on an
immeasurably large beach
amonst billions of star systems,
galaxies and even universes.
Please tell me there isn't a touch
of arrogance there?
STARSCAPE

Several messages there!
Physical confinement only
being one of them.
Psychology, Fear,
Desperation and
Frustration! .....
LET ME OUT

From Order to Chaos.
The way it works!
Next step: back to Order.
But there is no relative
time scale.
Only frequencies.
ENTROPY

Fear, Anxiety, Relief.
Fear, Anxiety, Relief.
Fear, Anxiety, Relief.
Get used to it!
BLOODSHOT

Where are we going?
Which is the stronger?
JUXTAPOSISION

Things were looking so gloomy
that we needed a boost
of positive energy.
The Wish is an etherial wave or
vibration that we all send out if
we think positively.
Delicate because it doesn't need
to be forceful!
Positivity is a vibration not a
physical object!
Fly with positivity, not drown with
negativity!
THE WISH

Middle of August 2020
When we started to get an idea
of what was really going on!
IGNITE

Can you see what is
happening?
Where are our borders?
When do they change?
Am I breaking the rules?
Well, what have you heard?
What's that barbed wire?
OUCH!

What by now we were desperate
for, was a bit of freedom.
After being kept in a virtual cage
for so long.
In the morning, we will look
on the bright side and
have a bright day!
;-)
DAWN KITES

There are so many rules and laws
and fears,
and they are changing constantly!
As soon as the fear wears off,
a new variant is "discovered".
And the fears and rules
are perpetuated.
And the coffers are filled
once more!
And, as usual, it's the ones who
can't afford, and most badly
affected who will end up
paying the price!
THE UNWRITTEN RULE

Seeing past the obvious!
Glimpses of the depth.
Inner workings of the power
struggle between what
we are told
and what, to me, was so
plain to see.
XRAY VISION

Family in different parts of the
world, but no way of getting to
see them, except via computer
video calls.
Everyone, it seems, being steered
towards technology.
Working from home.
Missing social time.
And now, banks closing face to face
branches, by the hundreds.
Pretty soon social interaction will
be a thing of the past.
TEARDROPS

Alison

In March 2020 my sister and her husband went off on their once in a lifetime dream holiday on a cruise around the Caribbean islands. They went for a month returning on the 26th of March and so missed the build up to lockdown.

I spent my time working, and cussing and cursing all those who were panic buying. I was down to one toilet roll and couldn't find any anywhere for love nor money. Food shortages were also doing my head in. I ranted on Facebook. Otherwise, life was pretty much normal.

I believed what the government and the media were saying but at the same time there was a little voice in my head saying something's not right. The voice had been whispering to me since February but it was so quiet I ignored it.

I was worried I would give this highly-infectious virus called covid 19 to my sister; she suffers from asthma and poly myalgia rheumatica so getting the virus could prove fatal. A week before my sister and brother-in-law were due back I cancelled all client appointments and stopped all unnecessary trips. Lockdown was then announced, and I couldn't go anywhere anyway.

I have a vegetable box delivered every week so I decided my sister could have that and I would go shopping after they got back. That way they didn't need to go shopping straight away and risk catching Covid 19.

I was so scared of giving my sister the virus I went shopping for myself the day after they returned from their holiday. I got to the supermarket and dutifully joined the queue outside, 6 feet behind the person in front. It all felt very surreal. A guy came and stood 2 feet behind me. As the queue moved the distance didn't change.

There was an old guy in front of me. His son came and joined him. The son looked to be in his early thirties, he could not stand still and kept encroaching on my space, which annoyed me. I heard him saying to his father that he needed the loo, which is probably why he couldn't stand still.

As they got to the front of the queue the flood gates opened and the son pee'd himself. He ran into the shop with wee still running down his leg and onto the ground. When I got to the entrance I reported the incident to the shop assistant on duty there who just replied "it's not my job to clean it up. I don't get paid danger money" and then laughed. I was both shocked and appalled and decided I wouldn't go back to that supermarket again!

Four days later I started to feel ill. I felt tired, had a headache and had developed a cough. I woke up the next day with a temperature and a horrendous all over body ache. My breathing was also tight. I could not sit, stand or lay down for long. The ache was so intense it was awful. I can remember cooking myself a meal and having a little accident with the herbs. When I ate the meal I could not taste the herbs and remember thinking I need to put more in next time as these seem to have lost their flavour. I was not ill for more than three or four days but the cough stayed with me for months and my eyesight took months to return to normal, as did my energy levels.

I worked as a bookkeeper/accountant and when we went into lockdown I thought I would be in for a quiet time as everything was shut. No sooner did I think that then the phone started ringing. My clients wanted to know what support was available and how they could go about getting it. I spent April and May buried in work, juggling my normal workload with keeping abreast of any newly available government funding. I had also taken on a new contract which kicked in at the end of April. I was busy!

I religiously watched the daily parliamentary covid updates and searched the government website for information on the available funding. I was too busy to listen to the little voice in my head that was still telling me something was not right.

By June work began to quieten down a bit and I started to take note of what was going on around me. I noticed that the case/death figures and descriptions given out in the media were changing; it didn't make sense to me.

A friend sent me a video by a bloke explaining how pandemics worked and how they lead to testemics, due to the increase in testing that is done, usually towards the end of a pandemic. It made a lot of sense to me and got me questioning things more. The voice in my head was no longer being ignored - it was being listened to.

I stopped watching mainstream media as it seemed very one sided, as did the one or two documentaries I saw, and there were not debates. I started searching the internet for information absorbing as much as I could. I went onto platforms and websites I'd never heard of before and followed people I previously didn't know existed. Friends sent me information and pointed me in various directions. The more I learnt the more appalled I was at what was going on.

At this stage I was still following the regime the government had set – mask wearing, social distancing, hand sanitising, etc. Part of me still believed in what they were saying but that part was shrinking rapidly with the more knowledge I gained. A lot of the rules that were being made and put into place overnight didn´t have any logic, didn't make any sense to me.

By the time the second lockdown came in November I was no longer watching the media or believing anything the government said. I still wore a face mask, as I hadn't plucked up the courage to leave it off, but I had stopped doing everything else. I hardly ever went anywhere where I had to wear a face mask anyway. I had never worn one when I went to see any of my clients.

When I tracked down and printed off an exemption card in May 2021 I stopped wearing a mask. The exemption card gave me the courage to do so. I now don't even consider putting one on.

The second lockdown, which started on the 5th of November 2020, hit me harder than the first, though it wasn't too bad. My workload was a lot quieter, and my birthday is in November.

I had started a course in the summer and was very disappointed that I had to put it down. My course involved learning how to work with animals' fascia muscles to ease chronic pain and as I do not have any pets and, because of lockdown, could not have access to other people's pets, it could not continue.

I began Christmas shopping early and started a couple of paintings which were to be given as Christmas presents. I also watched a lot of Christmas movies!

I was still doing research and information absorption, but not to the same extent - I was pleasantly distracted by Christmas and deadlines.

My birthday was two days after the start of lockdown. I had had an inkling that the country would be in lockdown again and so I had a plan B ready to be instigated if needed. I love picnics so, despite it being November and cold, I took myself off up to the top of the White Horse in the beautiful countryside of Wiltshire. I found a relatively quiet spot (which turned out to be a walkway) and had a picnic.

I sat there for the whole afternoon, getting a lot of strange looks from passers-by but I didn't care - it was lovely. I had so many layers on I didn't feel the cold. In fact, by the time I had walked to the top of the hill I looked like a beetroot .... I was so hot!

In the evening I went round to my sister and brother-in-law's (they are my support bubble) for a wonderful meal, wine and a movie. It turned out to be one of the best birthdays ever!

Despite government promises that we wouldn't be in lockdown over Christmas - we were!

I spent Christmas and Boxing Day morning with my sister and her husband; we had such a great time (at least I think so). It was so chilled and relaxed, with plenty of wine, good food and great company. We played Settlers, went for a walk and watched a movie or two. On Boxing Day I went home and had an indoor picnic by myself, and watched a movie. I was back round theirs for New Years Eve. More great food, wine, Settlers and a movie. We even managed to stay awake to see the New Year in - all of us looking forward to getting back to normal in 2021!

During the first quarter of 2021 things started to get tough for me emotionally; having spent so much of December with family I was now back on my own. The days were short, the weather was cold and money was tight. I was still researching and learning about the covid con. I only knew a couple of like-minded people.

The jabs were being rolled out, with promises of keeping us safe, being able to travel and getting back to normal, and my older relatives, my sister and a close friend queued up for theirs.

I couldn't tell them not to have them as I hadn't found my voice and I was scared of their reactions.

Instead I posted the links to the injection pages on the government website on Facebook; nobody looked at them. I sent information to people via Messenger and WhatsApp; they were ignored.

I started getting restless and frustrated. I posted more stuff on Facebook. I sent more links on WhatsApp, Messenger and Signal. Nothing was getting through. I felt alone, isolated in my beliefs and unable to talk to my friends or family as they had all bought into the narrative. There had to be more I could do.

I watched the first London protest on the various alternative channels. I shared some of the videos on Facebook. They were ignored. I knew I had to find my voice and I knew I had to go on a protest.

In May 2021 I went on my first protest ever. It was in Bath and I was very nervous. The protest was against the New Policing Bill that was going through the motions in parliament. I was against this Bill coming in as it was anti protesting, freedom of movement and freedom of speech. Masks had to be worn, which I didn't mind as it was against the Bill and not the covid restrictions. At the start of the protest there was a speech by the Green Party representative for Bath. This seemed odd to me and didn't sit well, but I later found out that there was a local election due.

Then when we started marching I saw a lady in front of me wearing a long black coat, at the bottom of the coat was written Extinction Rebellion and I knew then I was protesting with the wrong crowd. I stuck with it and did some videoing and joined in the chanting. Later that day I posted the videos on Facebook. I had found my voice.

The realisation that the health of my entire family, by this time they had all had at least one jab, all my clients and 98% of my friends could be affected seriously, that deaths could even occur over the next 2-3 years , if what the experts (the many from across the world who were not heard on the mainstream News) were saying is true.

I had already started noticing emotional, mental and physical changes in those that had been double-jabbed; in general the health of some of them had started to deteriorate.

I found myself sleeping more, drinking more and spending less and less time with the jabbed. I could not stop myself thinking about the consequence of what they had done to themselves. When they talked about their dreams and plans for the future I felt like crying as I did not believe they had a healthy future to look forward to. The sadness in me deepened. Even if they would listen I could not do that to them, they would be devastated. Instead I let them believe they have a future. At the moment they are happy and enjoying life. I can't say the same for me and it reminds me of that old saying 'ignorance is bliss'.

The sadness within me kept growing. I kept learning and researching. I learnt what the elite few were doing to the environment, that climate change was part of the agenda, that reducing the animal population worldwide was part of the agenda. I cried. I cried a lot during this time of realisation. The sadness I felt ran deep and throughout my whole body. It felt as if my soul was crying, not just for family and friends, but for the animals and plants – for the whole planet. This deep sadness lasted for a couple of weeks. I could not shed it. Then the sadness just went. It's as if my soul had cried itself dry and had learnt to accept (or found a way to live with) what was happening on this planet.

At the end of July 2021 I joined Stand In The Park Melksham and went back to protesting. This time with the right group of people. My family and friends know I am not jabbed and will not be. They do not like it but they are, for now, accepting it. I still feel sad when I meet my family and friends and see the changes in them caused by the jab. I know, deep down, that I will be saying goodbye to some of them within the next year. I try not to think of it as it just makes me cry. Instead, I try and find things to counteract the effects of the spike protein and encourage them to take them under the disguise of something else. I am also trying to find a way of helping all the animals who will find themselves homeless when their owners succumb to the effects of the jab.

With all this sadness and destruction around us I have to do what I can to bring light and positivity to the situation, to speak my voice and to help end this madness. It's the only way I can maintain my sanity and prevent me from spiralling into a deep depression that would end my life. I feel I still have a purpose. What that purpose is I do not know. I believe it will be revealed when the time is right.

"Never in my life have I wished so much that my belief in something was wrong."

Sam

It was March of 2020. The excitement that had buzzed around the student-led festival team with whom I work was beginning to be replaced by an unavoidable sense of dread; we had confirmed the booking of one of the biggest bands to ever perform at the music festival, but as COVID-19 reached the cities of the United Kingdom, the dream that the booking had carried with it was moving further and further away. It took a few more weeks for us to accept that the event would have to be cancelled, but even then, we didn't anticipate the extent to which the pandemic would continue to affect our lives.

Despite all this, the immediate impact of the pandemic on my personal life was not one of anxiety and stress, but one of tranquillity. In the months that led up to the pandemic, I had been living life at a million miles-an-hour; I had been working on the music festival, my own band, Demelza, were breaking into the local music scene, and I had been organising events for the student record label, all while pushing myself with my chemistry degree. Despite my unfaltering drive to give all these projects the best of myself, things all began to crumble as event dates came around and the ever-looming presence of exams crept nearer. All this meant that the pandemic felt like a helping hand when it arrived, like someone pressed pause on time to give me a chance to recoup.

Despite the masses of students around me rushing back to their family homes, I chose to stay at university for the first few months before I moved back home in May. Three friends of mine also decided to stay, two of whom were unable to move home due to vulnerable family members. We all moved in together, and the two months that followed blurred into one long, hazy summer's day. The area in which I had lived, normally bustling and chaotic, became serene. The pavements and parks were deserted, and the air was affectionate with the warmth of the sun. Where I could once hear a cacophony of building works and drunken shouting, I could now hear birdsong and the occasional wafts of music from open windows. It was exactly the break I needed, and a time that I look back on very fondly.

As a student in the pandemic, I'm very appreciative of my circumstances. While we lost a lot - our social lives, chunks of our education and most of our extracurriculars - we still had our student loans and the threat that COVID-19 posed to our own lives was relatively minimal. I'm very grateful for that, and I cannot begin to imagine the damage that the pandemic has wreaked on the lives of many others. I'm also very appreciative of my family, as I know not every student had a harmonious home to return to when the pandemic struck. The live music industry, despite being perhaps the hardest hit of all, continued to do what it does best: deliver inspiration and hope through its seemingly limitless ingenuity.

Musicians from all over the world streamed gigs from their back gardens, online festivals were organised, and some fantastic new music was released. Determined not to be defeated by the cancellation of our festival, we found motivation from the industry around us and worked on delivering the festival in a virtual format, all in the hope of raising money for the festival's charities. The support received by the festival was remarkable - more than twenty artists volunteered their time to produce virtual performances; the university radio station provided hosts for the stream and thousands tuned in to watch. None of us who worked on the event knew what to expect, so the sum of the donations received was truly astounding. While events like these punctuated the summer, they never shifted the view that live events would need to return at some point if the industry was to survive.

Each new lockdown was another step backwards and another punch in the gut to all those whose livelihoods depend on live events, especially as 70% of those working in music in the UK depend on freelance work, meaning they frequently fell between the cracks of the government's support plans. Seated gigs provided some respite for both those who work in the industry and for those for whom music is an important escape, but they acted as a mere plaster on a wound that needed surgery to truly heal.

As someone who both uses music both to escape and as a route through which I can find purpose, the loss of live music events inevitably began to take its toll on my wellbeing following my return to living at university in September. It had its hardest impact during the subsequent winter months of 2020, where the demands of my chemistry degree, which was mostly being conducted virtually, and the work on further online events arrived unaccompanied by the reward and rest that live events offer. My housemates and I did what we could to keep morale high - group dinners and game nights - but we were all very much in need of an escape by the time the Christmas holidays came around, even if we did have to spend most of the holiday revising for our exams.

I spent a long time at home before returning to university after Christmas, and I spent a lot of time by myself, which was very needed after being tangled up with my housemates for months on end. I read a book called Quiet by Susan Cain - one that changed the way I view myself and others, and one I especially recommend that anyone with any introverted characteristics reads.

When I did return, sometime towards the end of March 2021, things were beginning to open up a little, which allowed the festival team to begin optimistically planning a welcome back event for late June, a few days after the government planned for the complete removal of restrictions. While I'm not sure I ever truly believed the event would go ahead, it provided me with an impetus to throw myself back into the planning of events; it was exciting. We got painfully close - within two weeks of the day of the event - before it had to be cancelled. Still somewhat numb from all the previous cancellations, this didn't hurt too much, and my lasting feeling was of pride of what the team had achieved in the face of the pandemic. I think I also knew that, while we didn't quite make it with this event, the end was in sight, and for real this time.

As both a chemist and a music enthusiast, it's not often I find that these two worlds collide, but COVID-19 presented a time that chemistry produced a large part of the force that revived the live music industry. The depth, ingenuity and innovation in the research conducted across academia and industry throughout the pandemic is dumfounding; it shows the true magnitude of what can be achieved when the world puts its best minds together. I'm very grateful for all the work that has gone into ensuring as safe a return to social contact as possible, and for all those in the music industry, a return to doing what they do best.

I'm also proud of everyone else, throughout the country and the rest of the world, for not only enduring this period where so much was and still is being lost, but for coming together to produce the moments of beauty that have kept us going. There are countless examples of where small actions produced enormous results, illustrating the power of every individual. No one should ever doubt the positive impact they can produce themselves. I hope, and I believe, that we can overcome any crisis, whether it's COVID-19 or the climate crisis, if everyone does their part, however small it might seem.

Following another month of vaccine rollout, things finally opened again in late July, starting for me with a weekend at Latitude Festival in Suffolk. It was a truly beautiful reminder of what live music has to offer and why it had been such an important part of my life. I felt right at home and, judging by the thousands of smiles I was surrounded by all weekend, so did everyone else. The sun truly came out from behind the clouds that weekend, and while I don't know how long it'll remain that way, I'll make sure to enjoy every moment of it.

Pattie McGregor

Having been living on my own in Spain for many years, I was used to being in a quiet location and spending time doing whatever I wanted to do. I had the good fortune to be able to enjoy my freedom without having ties. This was very important to me as I had been a single parent, responsible for bringing up two sons in the UK on a very low budget, and often I had felt trapped.

To have my "freedom" in Spain was a great gift.

As of 4 March 2020 events took a very unexpected and dramatic change and so did my personal circumstances. I had taken a flight to the UK to attend my son´s special birthday celebration. Soon after my arrival I learned that Spain had gone into a very strict lockdown, due to a virus called Covid 19. The most shocking thing was when I heard that families were going to be kept indoors without having any exercise. I could not imagine a family being restricted inside a small flat with children without any kind of outdoor activity, my heart broke for them. The thought of being locked up in my apartment without proper daily exercise was a complete anathema to me!

Within a couple of weeks, it became obvious that England were also going to go into lockdown and the children would not be going to school. I am sure most people, like me, I believed it would only last a few weeks and then it would be over, it was very naive of me. It soon became clear that I had the choice to stay in England and help home school my grandchildren or return to Spain and live alone locked inside my apartment. As one of my careers had been as a teacher, the decision was not a difficult one and I knew my family would appreciate my help. Fortunately England allowed an hour's outside exercise per day along with a weekly visit to the supermarket and permission to walk a dog, if you had one. Spain, on the other hand, were still not allowing outdoor exercise, apart from a supermarket trip and a dog walk. Spain was also being very heavily policed with large fines being made to the "law breakers".

My son had always wanted me to live nearer to his family so that I could help them. His wish had finally come true. Not only was I actually living with him and his family every day, I was there to teach them and help in general!

So there I was again without my freedom. My feelings were however this time round very different, they were of strong gratitude.

1. I was living with my family while a strange "pandemic" was playing out.

2. I loved being with my grandchildren and felt very privileged to teach them.

3. I was there to actually see my grandchildren growing and changing and have fun with them.

4 I could get some outside exercise every day.

5. I could watch Netflix! (I didn't have it in Spain).

6. I was still able to have communication with my friends in Spain.

I did miss the quiet of my apartment as the family's house was close to a busy road. I had to adapt to living with four other people, just as they had to get used to me being there.

As it happened, I stayed 4 months to the day before I flew back to Spain.

As a spiritual person, I had a lot of trust in the Universe and my angels, and I had learned to follow my intuition. I soon realised that I had been "put" in the best place for me and my family. When I had booked the flight to Spain, I had only booked a single which I had never done before and I couldn't understand why I felt so reluctant to book the return. Thank goodness for my gut feeling.

To date, the "pandemic" and lockdowns have been a huge spiritual lesson for me and I have been so fortunate to have felt very little fear and much anticipation of the happiness that is ahead for the human race as we ascend into the Golden Age.

Jimmy

Las Vegas - February 2020 - enjoying a cocktail whilst watching gamblers in the casino below, when everything stopped and an announcement was made on a huge TV screen.

The gambling machines came to a grinding halt and the gamblers were not amused, infact they were angry; they listened to the news and then carried on regardless. They appeared unaffected by the announcement they had just heard and everything was immediately in full swing again - the noise, the gambling, the expectant, happy, and disappointed faces; all at different stages of winning or losing money!

The announcement that had just been made on the big screen was "BREAKING NEWS - coronavirus sweeps America. CDC Says COVID-19 Is Heading Toward Pandemic Status". I felt that this was something we should all be pretty worried about but that wasn´t the word or the feel on the streets of Las Vegas in the days that followed.

I wasn´t hearing people talking about this virus that was "sweeping America". I was really surprised at the apparent no reaction of the people I saw and met. I heard on many occasions people expressing how pleased they were to have Trump as President to see them through whatever was happening. I was really shocked; in Europe I had only ever heard and seen people making fun of Trump. This made me realize how much influence the media have on portraying public figures and people mainly believe what they see and read.

I spent a month travelling in and around Columbus, Georgia and Savanah with a friend, socialising, meeting and chatting to other visitors and locals. I never saw anyone in a mask and the impending threat of the virus was not being spoken about at that time. Everyone and everything appeared very relaxed, nothing had changed and I got swept along in a false sense of security and carried on enjoying my holiday.

I finally flew from Georgia to London Heathrow. No-one wore a mask on the plane and the flight was full. On arriving at Heathrow I was shocked to see people in masks; I saw fear for the first time, it was like landing in another world. There were constant public announcements about the virus.

Having come from a busy but totally normal airport in the States, Heathrow felt like a frenzy, the tension was tangible; people in masks, people hand sanitising. I was shocked and thought "what the hell have I come back to".

I got a coffee and watched successive flights arriving from China which I thought was interesting in view of the fact we were being told the virus had originated in China.

When I got home and started watching the BBC news it was showing horrific scenes from Italy, people dying in hospital corridors, and people dropping dead on the streets in China. The news from Spain was pretty alarming too.

Since then 18 months have passed and we have heard different news from the different States in America. I have kept in touch with American friends and the news we have heard in the UK has not always been the same as how they have described their eveyday lives.

Karl

So, lockdown…where do I start? I embraced it for what it was, the means of preventing a deadly respiratory virus from ravaging the UK population. I was that pragmatic and eager user of latex gloves in the supermarket, that eventual wearer of masks and the overzealous user of "highly effective" antibacterial handwash whenever the Amazon driver dropped a package at my door. This virus was not catching me.

I would be dodging it like I dodged the kid who was 'it' in a game of school tag. See you later Corona!

I never voted for Boris Johnson. I can't stand the man, but I found I was hanging on his every word, not out of fear, but more because I was gripped with what was happening. SARS-CoV- 2 seemed to unite us all against one enemy. Brexit what?

At the start of lockdown in March 2020 I was quite breezy about things. An Englishman's home is his castle, right? For now, let's ignore the fact I am half English and half Welsh. I was spending my time on my work, walking the dog, relaxing in the hot tub with a glass of wine and gazing up at the stars at every opportunity, only to have it ruined when I saw Elon Musk's satellites sweeping across the beautiful night sky! I was also keeping a keen eye and ear on the news.

Whitty and Co were keeping me updated on key topics such as daily death tolls, asymptomatic spread and they explained this virus had a 14-day incubation period before it would come out of its murky hiding place in our bodies. I was so appreciative for their input, I really was. They were spoiling me with their years of medical knowledge and when I was finally allowed to see my parents in person in an outdoor space it was comforting knowing that by keeping two metres away from them and not hugging them, I was being a good citizen and potentially saving their lives. Ill until proven healthy. That was the assumption.

As time went on from the start of lockdown my patience and resolve started to dwindle and those once-loveable weekly Zoom calls with friends weren't quite hitting the high notes they did a few weeks before. There is only so much online fancy dress or topical quizzes I can take in one lifetime. Something was missing and lockdown started to grind me down: the combination of a lack of social interaction and close contact with friends and family; the inability to dine in restaurants; visit a cinema; drink beer in a pub garden on a sunny afternoon. I couldn't head to the gym and pretend to enjoy lifting weights whilst pulling strange faces. I missed these things, and it was starting to take its toll. I needed to distract my mind.

I started by throwing myself into an old childhood hobby and I built an intricate radio-controlled car. It became an obsession and I would find myself up at 3am soldering wires together frantically like a mad professor. I like to do things to the best of my ability and I hate to fail at certain things – not all things. I liked the precision that was required to build this thing. It was a challenge. I only used it about ten times before I sold it. Some hobbies should just be left in the past.

One release was getting out on my mountain bike and I found I was riding a lot on the country roads local to me. I started to feel a little disgruntled when I was being passed by those lycra cladded bike wankers (hey, I didn't invent that term!). Who the hell do they think they are, gliding past me effortlessly with a few turns of their crank. In light of this it made perfect sense that I buy my own road bike. I am now said lycra cladded bike wanker, with the wardrobe to prove it! If you can't beat them, join them and if I am being completely honest, wearing lycra isn't so bad after all. I will stop there before I say too much.

My road bike transformation wasn't quite complete, however. My bike was an endurance bike and it was too heavy. I wanted something lighter, more nimble and with better technology. What can I say, I'm a techno-cock! (My cousin coined that term back in '06.) I took it upon myself to build my own bike so I could learn how to repair and service my bikes in the future and also to save some money. The bike I built was a thing of beauty. I am far less materialistic than I used to be, but I appreciate beautifully engineered parts, aerodynamic features and stunning looks. The electronic shifters are magnificent. Like I said, techno-cock.

My older brother, Jim, has been a big influence on me of late. I remember about 8 years ago at my cousin's house he showed me the collapse of Building 7. You know, that building next to the World Trade Centre, the one that wasn't hit by a plane. It collapsed in on itself, just like that. Some might say it looked like a controlled demolition. I was shocked at the time. It was clear to me what happened. I have eyes and I do not consider myself to be someone without intellect. Still, time passed and I forgot about it, until recently.

Early in 2021 my brother, Jim, started to tell me how he had stopped wearing a mask in the shops. I was impressed at his boldness. How did he manoeuvre those insistent mask-enforcing supermarket workers? I wanted to know more. It stirred something in me, my rebellious side. My brother was telling me about his meetups with other like-minded people in open spaces. It made me think and I started to humour my brother, not from a place of condescension, but from a place of intrigue. Why is he meeting with these people? What is the point of all this?

Jim started to talk me through the information he had read, and videos watched of medical and pharmaceutical experts, people I hadn't seen on the BBC News. People who were suggesting everything Boris and Co had explained to us about Covid weren't quite as they seemed. My mind started working overtime, as it does.

Jim then sent me the game changer - Planet Lockdown's Mike Yeadon interview. This ex-Chief Scientific Officer of Pfizer was completely tearing apart the mainstream narrative on Covid in an experience-driven, intelligent, thought-provoking and easy-to-understand series of explanations of his grave concerns. Within the space of 60 minutes my thinking had shifted completely and everything the Government had told me was starting to feel, look and smell like a massive lie. I was alarmed, confused and worried.

Off the back of this interview I requested more information from by brother, which he gladly obliged. I could tell my brother was relieved and happy that he was able to wake me from a place of hypnosis. I was too. From this point onwards I can say I went further and further down the rabbit hole.

It's probably a good time to tell you that I was engaged to marry my fiancé in August 2020. Well, now ex-fiancé. At the time of the first lockdown we were living together in my house in a small village outside Bedford and, due to Covid, we weren't able to get married, which looking back now was a blessing in disguise. Our relationship wasn't as strong as what it once was. Perhaps, if I am being honest, it was never as strong as I hoped for. The lockdowns didn't help us. The isolation took away our ability to do the things we enjoyed doing together - activities that normally led us into a false sense of security that our relationship was a healthy one. We were now spending 24/7 together in the house and I felt this exposed not only the flaws in our relationship, but also our incompatibility.

Among many attributes I look for in a partner, one I yearn for is that conversational spark, the ability to talk and debate effortlessly about a whole range of subjects: important or damn right silly. Unfortunately, I just didn't have that with my ex and it's not to say she wasn't capable of it. I simply feel we weren't capable of it with each other. We also argued and clashed a lot and I started to feel we didn't have as much in common as we had hoped.

Despite this, I didn't want to give up – perhaps she felt the same, or maybe she wasn't aware of how I was feeling. We decided to buy a house together, to invest in our relationship and also to take advantage of the 0% stamp duty that was available due to the Government's monetary relief. Some people make babies to try and fix a relationship. Perhaps this was us making a baby.

We moved to West Oxfordshire on 2nd March 2021 and it wasn't long after this that my brother had shared his insights with me and I had my eureka moment. The covid vaccines had started to be rolled out 4 months earlier and I started to hear in the press about people dying from blood clot related complications following their vaccination, which was worrying, especially as I remember saying to my fiancé in August 2020 that I couldn't wait for a vaccine to be created so we could all get "back to normal". You know the phrase, it's been pumped out in the mainstream media countless times, along with their other slogans and sound bites. I feel quite naïve now looking back at how I believed the government wholeheartedly, without doing any additional research on people who were challenging the narrative. That has been a huge issue with this whole "pandemic". There has been no debate!

At this point, after speaking more to my brother I had also stopped wearing masks when out on my own. With my mind shifting the way it was, knowing now that I would not be having any experimental, still-on-trial-until-2023, mRNA spike protein producing, blood clot inducing vaccines, I envisaged a rocky road ahead for myself and my fiancé.

In order to keep the peace with her I begrudgingly carried on wearing a mask for her, at her request, in her presence to make her feel better. One of the biggest problems I started to have with her was her constant worry about what others thought about her; it consumed her and it wasn't healthy. On one occasion I walked through the pub with her from the pub garden to the street. I had had a few pints and I was feeling bold so I took my mask off as we walked through the pub. I was later told that she was embarrassed to be seen with me when I didn't wear my mask.

Imagine that, your own fiancé is too concerned about what others think and is embarrassed for others to see her partner's face. I was told I was being "selfish." That old chestnut!. It upset me and it started to feel like the beginning of the end.

My ex was 100% committed to getting vaccinated so she could "do her bit to help get things back to normal", "go on holiday", keep herself "safe from covid" and to "help protect others". It was sad to see the person closest to me regurgitating all of the government's propaganda messaging back at me when I just didn't believe their motives were pure. We had many tense and horrible arguments about these vaccinations, mainly because I expressed a deep concern about them from the alternative sources I had read and she just was not interested in sharing my concerns.

At first she was concerned about my health and told me Covid could hit me hardest because I have asthma. I believe she was genuinely concerned, I really do, but I explained it's only light asthma, I cycle a lot and the survival rate for people under 70 was 99.95%. She then at a later date told me that we would not be able to go on holiday together. I asked her if she thought it was madness that unvaccinated people would not be allowed to travel freely across borders due to a virus with such a low death rate, to which she proudly expressed that this is "the new normal".

I was crying inside and I felt I was being emotionally pressurised to do something I did not want to do. I tried to show her peer reviewed information I had read and watched from well-renowned medical and pharma experts who were opposing the mainstream view and she was just not interested in spending any time with me to at least understand why I was so worried.

Three and a half years together and she couldn't even be bothered to spend one evening with me to look at this information. That's all I wanted, her time to listen to my worries, but it fell on deaf ears. She was trying to convince me that we could have a different opinion on this and still be fine, but deep down I just knew this wouldn't work.

She came back one day and said she had done some research, which made me hopeful. She then followed up by explaining she had done her research on which vaccine she was going to take. It saddened me that someone this smart wasn't even prepared to challenge her own assumptions, her own way of thinking.

From this point I felt a sad emptiness when I looked into her eyes and I remember the exact point where I knew I no longer wanted to be with her. We went to a pub a few miles away from where we live. It was the first time we could go into a pub after the early 2021 lockdown, there was no one outside but she took out her mask, put it on and dutifully scanned the QR code on the door with her NHS app, an app I have never downloaded, may I add! I actually felt sorry for her and how she had been brainwashed into such a compliant and fearful state. This was no longer someone I wanted to spend my life with and our relationship ended two days later.

Whilst there have been understandably and expectedly some negatives during these last 18 months, I would say that I have been fortunate to experience more profound positives as a result of these lockdowns. I always try to focus on the positives.

I didn't mention it earlier, but before March 2020 I was all ready to set up a new car detailing business, which would have locked me into a career that would have made me miserable and been a complete disaster. Covid saved me from this. I avoided a marriage that was destined to fail. Covid strikes again!

I was able to relocate to West Oxfordshire, which is a beautiful part of the UK, right on the edge of the Cotswolds, which is great for cycling and brings me closer to the South West. This has proved a fantastic move for many different reasons.

However, whilst these are all perfectly tangible benefits, they do not compare to the more profound positive changes that I have experienced within myself. I have learnt to challenge the mainstream narrative and my own way of thinking. Nothing is quite what it seems and I shouldn't be relying on the Government and large corporations for the news that matters. I feel with all this research I have engaged my brain in a way I haven't for a number of years. I feel I can debate my points more intelligently, provide clear rationale and back myself up with factual information. Of course, I don't expect everyone to share the same views as me and many would regard me as a conspiracy theorist and an anti-vaxxer.

Everyone is entitled to their own opinion no matter how much you disagree with them. In conversations with people on this matter I have found I have also become calmer when speaking with those who are unable to converse in a rational and calm way. This has also been an extremely refreshing change in how I conduct myself.

Through all of this I have grown far closer to my brother and his wife in a way that I could have never imagined. I was close to my brother before, but this shared common interest has formed a bond between us that was unexpected, yet massively appreciated.

This has meant I have spent far more time with my beautiful niece and I have been able to grow my understanding of her and her of me.

During the last 6 months on my journey of waking up and smelling the bull shit I have met and spoken to many people who share the same thoughts as me with regards to this "pandemic". I have made many new friends with people I click with instantly and for that I am grateful.

So, what are my hopes for the future? At a macro level I simply want this whole fraudulent "pandemic" to be exposed for what is really is – a PCR plandemic, which is being driven and orchestrated by corrupt governments and corrupt corporate organisations.

Reiner Fuellmich – we stand by you and your legal work and we hope you and your colleagues and associates around the world can expose this for what It really is – a massive fraud. If this can be done I feel like the normal everyday activities can resume as before March 2020.

Unfortunately, my worries lie with all of these millions of people who have been psychologically brainwashed by their governments and made to be fearful of something that is no more harmful than the flu. If they do come to realise they have been completely duped into participating in the world's largest ever clinical trial there will be the type of mass soul searching taking place that we have never seen before.

I really hope that the opposing sides predictions of mass deaths over the next 2-3 years because of these vaccinations blood clotting properties are untrue. If the predictions are true and many die, I hope my parents, family and close friends have had the placebo.

Ultimately, I am hopeful I am wrong about all of this. I would quite happily swallow my pride and admit to all those who think I have gone mad that I have been wrong about everything.

Bringing it back to the masses, whether I am right or wrong, many people have suffered needlessly with these lockdowns through losing their businesses, losing their jobs, being unable to have time critical operations. Mental health and suicides have shot through the roof and I feel all of these people have been completely forgotten and neglected during this horrible period. I just want their suffering to end.

As for my hopes for my own future, I want to continue to travel down the new path that has been carved for me in terms of personal growth. This includes challenging the mainstream narrative, challenging my own assumptions, building new friendships, keeping old friendships, continuous learning and development, laughter and enjoying the UK (and rest of the world, if that is ever possible) for all its wonders in my new campervan. I want to continue the adventure wherever it takes me.

I'm happy in my own skin, I have a lot to give and I now know what I am looking for in a partner; I hope to meet a beautiful and amazing soul who I can share my life with. I don't think that is too much to ask for in such a crazy and upside-down world.

Deborah Sutton

*"I follow my joy to raise my frequency,
I share it with others to raise theirs."*

Our creative power lies in our ability to choose our beliefs

Aisling Mary Melchizedek

As the lockdown hit, I was so fortunate to have my youngest son here as he had just a couple of days earlier come over from Switzerland to visit me, so it was wonderful to have his company throughout all these 10 weeks.

Initially we followed a little bit of the news to see which narrative was been sold to humanity and we became aware very soon that half or more of what the mainstream media was sharing was not right and that it was all being made up so we would enter fear and anxiety. I realized very fast that this was part of a plan that was already made up many years prior and was part of the agenda 2030.

With the research we began doing and as time went on, it was confirmed that there was a genocidal plan behind the story and that all they try is to fully control and brainwash humans, to lower their vibrations and immune systems so people would be easier to manipulate, to then begin to implement that injection beginning with V, which under no circumstances is a V but a lethal injection modifying our genetics and DNA, containing RNA messengers and more, which are connected to the 5G Towers which have been put up all over the world as we were in lockdown, and once they will be turned on, we will see masses dying, which then will result in increased numbers and lockdown again blaming these deaths on the youngsters to have spread the fake Virus and its fake variants again, trying to hide the truth about the Injection, thinking we are all so stupid to believe that nonsense they are selling us.

That has always been their plan, a reduction of humanity by giving that injection to all, that shot is full of poison and particles harming us and stopping us to fully evolve and ascend into higher Dimensions, severing the emotional body from the Soul so we become robotic and are fully controllable and they can manipulate us and use our energies as they like, turning us into their Slaves. When I say they, I mean the Deep state, do your own research, and find out about the truth, take only what resonates with you and leave the rest.

I soon understood the complexity and reasoning behind it all and the control Agenda being covered up with lies and manipulations. This all made me stand up and really stand in my power as not to follow nor believe any of this BS and act as a Sovereign Being that we are by birth I refused to wear a mask on the road and smiled to each one once lockdown finished that crossed my path, looking at me in disbelief as I wasn't wearing a mask. I literally made myself invisible and each day when I went out, I set that intention.

There were many days, when a police car drove past me, not seeing me at all. It was such a pleasure to go against all the implemented rules. At nights after curfew hours I went for walks to the seaside, enjoying the peace and quiet hours of the night. I was happy that Nature in these weeks could recuperate itself from all we do to her, the animals were active, the dolphins came back into the Bay, the birds sounded louder and that needed break was helping Mother Earth to eliminate all these toxins we humans carelessly put in and on her. This all was so beautiful to observe and feel.

Also, the fact that families got more united despite the physical separation they had to go through; the opportunity for each human to connect within themselves and see all the potentials lying within, the chance to look at the shadows we all carry and clear them, taking time to do things we long have wanted to do but not found the so-called time to do them.

When we understand that time is just an illusion and another form of control we were indoctrinated into and we understand that it is each now moment we live, things change. Our perception changes. We begin to expand in Consciousness.

All this is what I accepted to see, recognize, feel, and live, leaving behind all negative components of that time, jumping timelines quantically and being very grateful for it and all the opportunities we were given to change and look within us Stopping to live only an external, superficial life with addictive consumption habits, totally disconnected from our essence, wanting to possess and have all the material items possible. Completely forgetting that we have come to this planet with a higher purpose, mission, and huge spiritual abilities to develop.

Many nights in the times of lockdown, we played loud music on our terrace and connected with Neighbours in other Buildings nearby, who began asking us by shouting out loud the song they wanted to be played, and my son, who was the Disc Jockey on our terrace, played their songs. We had such fun and loved it all. We loved the way humans united in these times worldwide in their own ways possible.

I began sending so much light and love into each part of the world with energy and light codes, anchoring them into the Core of Mother Earth daily, so they could light the Earth grids and humans could then benefit from it to keep themselves strong.

These times we are in, are tough on many and you should know that it is in fact a War, one that is being played out on all levels.

I cannot state enough to each one who reads these words to stand strong and hold on to all that is happening and will still happen, remain neutral, detach from all media and its news to avoid your energies to lower, to trust that all will be sorted and that all these old structures and controlling systems must collapse for us to create the new.

We must all remember that this has got a higher purpose, to bring all humanity into the Awakening since we are in the Ascension phase, for all to see, what has been done with us for millions and millions of years, we are breaking out of the prison planet now that the Gates have opened for us to change Densities. The Gates have been closed for so long, each 26.000 years only do they open and remain open for 4.600 years where all Souls must ascend.

Much more will be soon revealed and come to the surface for all to see as how many lies and manipulation has been done here to all. Many Souls are already leaving now and will continue in the coming months/years as the injection is beginning to show its effects. A lot is happening, things we can't even imagine, it will be very painful for many. We must remember that many Souls have taken on contracts to help humanity ascend from the other side, and that is perfectly fine so.

When we learn to change our Consciousness and accept that there is so much we do not even know, and simply allow for all to flow in its divine time and happenings, sending love to all, blessing all and detaching emotionally from it all being in neutrality, we see the bigger picture and understand with a lot of compassion and without judgement.

Standing up now, remembering that we are God, we are Sovereign, and we are Free, we create this New Earth where there no longer will be control nor manipulations, where we all together help each other, sharing all we need and have, not depending on any Government, Politicians, Health Systems, not any other fake structure that is only abusing us humans and our rights in all ways possible, making us dependent on them. We will be living amazing lives, growing our own healthy food, using medicine plants, alternative remedies, and energy work as healing tools only for our wellbeing, fully in alignment with Nature and Mother Earth, reconnecting to our Senses and our high potential that we all have come here with by default, but have forgotten to use them because of all these conditionings and limiting beliefs we are educated into.

We are returning to our Divine Knowledge, leading the way forward as Way Showers so all can follow and know we are all divinely guided and sustained and protected, each one according to their own individual plan, when we follow our calling, strong and fearless.

I hope this story resonates with you and helps and inspires you to stand up for your rights, for all humans, collectively. Do all you can to maintain your Body, Mind and Soul in Harmony and Balance and we shall see us all at the other end of new, marvelous beginnings of this amazing New Earth.

After all, we all who are here now, chose to be here, to in whatever form, help raise the Planet into its highest potential and vibration.

Jill from Noosa, Australia

The start of my Covid journey was blessed by a trip to Hawaii swimming with dolphins and at a spiritual retreat at the beginning of March 2020..... As my sister and I chatted to the locals about this "flu thing" that was going on in the world, many of them thought they had already had it as they'd experienced a severe flu like illness and an enduring cough and felt worse than they had done in years, but were now recovered. The town of Kona, on the Big Island of Hawaii seemed in a complete bubble from the news that started emerging over our two week stay. Ten days in having spoken to family back home in Australia I Informed some of my fellow retreaters that we may have to isolate on arrival.home. I remember how we all laughed and my sister joked likening it to an AA meeting saying "Hello my name is........ and I'm a self isolater" We had no comprehension of the journey that 18months later we would still be in the middle of.

We took one of the last flights out of Hawaii. We both decided to self isolate at my sister's with her husband who also volunteered to isolate with us, whilst my husband did the shopping for us which he deposited at the front door and we only talked over the fence for two weeks. My grown up children who lived locally felt it was all too weird to not be able to touch so we just spoke on the phone. It was the first time in years we weren't all together for my son's birthday; he posted a photo on Facebook of his Covid party - him in an empty room pretending to dance by himself.

My sister's house is light and spacious and living in Queensland, Australia we were blessed with nice weather and a swimming pool in the back garden. We decided to carry on our retreat and meditated daily, swam our allotted lengths, did our vibro plates and wondered at the news everyday comparing the stories we were hearing from family and friends all over the world, still naively thinking this would all be over in a few weeks.

Going out after isolation was strange and confronting. I wasn't sure of all the rules of social distancing and what you were and weren't allowed to do and my main concern was not to do anything that would make people feel uncomfortable; I work as a disability support person so have very vulnerable clients and needed to make sure I didn't compromise them in any way. From a personal point of view I have never had a fear of catching the Covid but I began to realise how differently this "thing" was affecting everyone. People's reactions were really surprising me.

Having not seen one of my closest friends for a couple of months she made it clear we would not be hugging, ok I respected that, if that made her more comfortable, but when I did visit she reminded me that I hadn't washed my hands and as I did so she started singing Happy Birthday! I thought how sweet of her seeing as she had missed my birthday, but then I realised that wasn't the case at all, she was singing it twice because that was the recommended thing to do to make sure you washed your hands for the correct length of time. I was so shocked - here was someone I'd always felt so close to acting like I was a potential threat to her wellbeing, I found it hard to believe why she seemed so distant and it made me feel like I didn't really know her.

As the time has passed, I have spent many hours researching all avenues and reconnected with old friends. I have been surprised by different friends, family and acquaintances´ views. I have heard some wonderfully encouraging stories about people's kindness to their fellow man and also some heartbreaking stories of people being unable to see their families, losing their businesses, suffering from depression.....to me so much of what is going on doesn't make any sense.

Some of the rules of lockdown, mask wearing and quarantine are truly unbelievable. When you get people not allowed to see their dying child but all the football teams or movies stars are allowed to enter the state because of money.....urgh ......makes me angry.

As with everything in life we have all travelled different roads and had different experiences that lead us to make our decisions. For me the biggest message is to be respectful of others views and opinions, no way do I want to fall out with my dearest friends and family over matters that none of us will probably ever really know the whole truth about.

I learnt a long time ago that LOVE is always the answer and no other time more than now do I need to practise this.

Sending love.

Janet Jackson Tyler Lummer

"Where do I begin to tell the story of how great a love can be. A sweet love story that is older than the sea, the simple truth about the love she brings to me, Where do I start"

These are the lyrics that came to my mind when you asked for my covid time story.

My love for life, my love for my family, my love for my fellowman, all this is what covid time is all about. Where does your loyalty lie when it comes to life or death? Who do you believe when it comes to life or death? Where is your moral compass?

Those are all the questions that came to me as I have navigated this time and treasured this time and dreaded this time. My biggest personal concern is how was I going to be able to support my son and myself if my industry (entertainment)does not start working again? What happens if I get sick with the virus, I will also not be able to work. As a freelance artist or business owner these are our concerns. But the fact of having to deal with the trust issue of what to believe was the most aggravating maddening sad angry feelings I have ever felt in my life. Sometimes I felt my head was just spinning with too much information and I just could not keep up with it. Every day there was something new to consider. And then on top of it, WHAT should I believe !!!!!!

What I did know is my Mother had told me never to take a flu shot because she took the Hong Kong flu shot for precaution and she almost died. She became paralyzed and my Father had to take care of us and it was a horrible nightmare, and that is when she told me not to take these flu shots, so I have not taken one in my life and I have not had the flu my entire life. So when this vaccine shot came up I was totally against taking it, because of what I promised my Mother years ago. The Hong Kong flu was also killing people, and there was a choice to make, so knowing what happened to my Mother I stood my ground and said I will not take it. I do not need it, my immune system is great I will wear my mask and keep my distance and I will be fine. I truly believed this and felt comfortable with my decision. I also was not traveling and I do my work from my home always, so being at home was not unusual and going to the store and the bank were my outings.

As time passed and we were getting to my age group here in Alicante, Spain I had not been called to get a vaccine. I was happy about it, because it had seemed they had forgotten about me, and I would laugh and say "oh it is good to be a foreigner, they do not care if we get the vaccine or not...." then my son who is 21 kept asking me if someone has called me yet, because all his friends parents are getting vaccinated. He knew I did not want to get one, but he just kinda ignored talking about it to me. He knew I was waiting to see what would happen to people that are taking it, but not really understanding that I did not want to take it no matter what is happening to other people. Hence:The side effects. My family in the States were taking it and everyone in my family had no problems with it not 1, and we are 100's. I had cousins that they felt they already had covid before it was called a pandemic but just did not know it. They just remember that they were really sick for months and then they finally got better so they said they were immune to it and they were not going to take the vaccine, and they never have, and they are fine.

Then my son came in one day and sat with me and said "Momma you need to take the vaccine. I am afraid every day that I can come home and maybe give it to you because I am out more than you." I protect myself and do what I am suppose to do, but you never know I could get it and it will be horrible if you catch it and get sick. (His Father died when he was 13) I just can not live with this feeling of fear everyday." He had tears in his eyes, and at that moment I knew I had to take the vaccine because my loyalty is to my son's well-being and it broke my heart to know he was living in fear all this time and did not say it in hopes someone was going to call me and I could get the vaccine, but the phone never rang.

So I called the Centro de Salud and the first thing they said was "We have been looking for you, but the number we had was wrong !!!!!!" Well I had changed my number over 1 year ago, but I thought they had it, but they did not. So in 3 days I had an appointment and I have now had both of my Pfizer shots. Had no major side effects whatsoever. But by waiting I had a lot more information that I would not have had had I taken the vaccine earlier. Learning what was the best vaccine for me to take, what I should do physically after I have the shot, and what to know about the different side effects. This was wonderful information to have. At one point I was given information about should I take paracetemol before and after I get the shot theory. I had 3 medical doctors advice me and all 3 had a completely different idea about the situation. One said "take 30 minutes before the shot, then again 2 hours after having the shot". other said, "You will not need anything, they just tell that to people that are asking too many questions so they say to take these pills just to calm you down" . The last said "IF you feel not well, then take something" All I could do was laugh, and I just took nothing. I had different little feelings, but not enough to have to take anything for it. I chose the road " When in doubt, do nothing" I am not a pill taker anyway, so I followed my mind.

When going to the clinic I arrived at the door and said I was here for my covid vaccine appointment. They asked for no ID, no paper that showed I had an appointment, just said "Go to room 6" so went to room 6 and gave my name, again no one asked for ID, so I could have been anyone off the street coming in to get MY shot. I found that amusing and scary at the same time. This is supposed to be so important and you do not even know who you are really giving this shot to, because none of you know me. So just to say, it was very easy to receive my shot here in Spain. No complications whatsoever.

My son is relieved and I know in the end God will protect me through all of this and I have no fear at all about my decision to put my love for my son first. My son being happy is what makes me happy and happy people are healthy people because it keeps the immune system up and that is where we are.

So my questions I asked at the beginning of my letter have been answered. My love for my family is where my loyalty and moral compass lie. They are my life and that is why I love life, and if I have to die because of them, I will do it a thousand times with no regret.

Love you dearly Rosanne.

Always In Spirit,
Janet Jackson Tyler Lummer

P.S.

In terms to our futures on this planet. WOW where do I start.....
There is so much that can happen for us that can be incredibly
AMAZING and POSITIVE and THAT is what I am praying for.
Us as human beings, learning to respect one another's choices
in life, and also realizing how your choices affect others and
being mindful about it and putting yourself in their shoes. Greater
communication between us all by asking questions about things
you do not understand and really wanting to understand so there
can be harmony in our world. Seeing what needs to be changed
in the world and REALLY changing things completely. Not just
starting something and then in 6 weeks we never hear about it
again. Having a MAJOR NEW NEWS Network (called (NFG)
CHANGE FOR GOOD) that speaks on the matters in the world
that must be faced and changed and the programs and people
that are making the changes. Having them on everyday to let us
,the public , know what is happening each and every day and all
results and conclusions. Reporters that stay on the story until it
is completely DONE. Separate videos that keep us up on all the
stories that you can check in on to see the progress of the day on
that particular story which you are interested in. Things change
when people are talking about it and being active. Most changes
occur when we are willing to die for them, and fear leaves the
room. I would much rather die for a cause then a disease !!!!!!!!!
HOWEVER: death is not necessary if we Honor and Trust each
other through Love and Grace.

AMEN

Kristin Kalnapenk, Estonia

The first time I heard about the "deadly virus" it seemed to be somewhere far away in China. I had freshly started pole dance lessons in January 2020. I fell in love with how both, the tough male and the gracious female energy are represented in pole dance. So I bought a pole for home. On that day everything closed down and my group trainings were over. I started following and learning from dancers I saw on instagram and greatly enjoyed my time at home. We were sent home from university as well - I study jazz in the Estonian Academy of Music and Theatre - and I suddenly had so much time on my hands and I could make my own schedule without restrictions. I was powered up, made great progression in pole dancing and wrote a lot of songs/ideas.

I had recently started a body cleansing juice feast of 35 days, and with the extra energy I had from not digesting, and the lighter my body was, the progression I made in strength was massive for me. I was in a good place mentally and physically to be alone and decide for myself, it was okay for me to have no teachers or not too much social life because I was so eager to learn and progress in my own pace.

The nature was of big help and relief as well - I ran and meditated every day in the forest next to my home. This helped me to stay focussed.

Summer came around and public places opened up. Being in a studio where all three aerial sports were represented, I also tried out the aerial hoop. With a base of pole dance of 10 months, I had one month to apply my skills for the hoop, because I had my first fully produced concert of my own music with a full band coming up and I thought it would be cool to use an element of aerials on the show. As pole dancing seemed to be too extreme for a university theatre, I chose to work on the hoop. In a month I learned what I could and did my performance with utmost enthusiasm during a song of mine called "Sexual Energy". The concert turned out amazing, it was sold out but sadly people were afraid to come and it ended up being only half full.

I also had an interesting experience on TV, where I made it to the semifinals on the pre contest for Eurovision. Usually the biggest concert hall of Estonia would be crowded with people but this time there was nobody in the audience but the rest of the competitors. We had to wear masks in the corridors and it was a feeling of unfairness I hadn't felt before in my country. I hadn't been suppressed by the government to do something before in my life.

But the summer of 2021 Estonia was pretty chill about the rules and we could enjoy our summer to the fullest. Then the vaccine party started and now I thank God I'm surrounded by like-minded people who care about the planet, humanity's wellbeing and our own experiences in this life. My friends own a beautiful vegan restaurant where they have live music and which is a private territory owned by the wealthiest awoke businessman in Estonia and we don't have to worry about the government disturbing our peace. Apart from that place, as for now (2021 September) it's not allowed go to restaurants or social gathering places without a covid pass. So Restaurant Oasis is the only place we can hang out or have dinner.

I'm curious to see what will happen next and I wonder how the mess will be solved and if it ever will. The schools are starting slowly to close down again. I'm afraid there will be a great fall at some point, but till then, all we can do is our best for ourselves and the loved ones.

Joe Hellyer-Gallagher

"This music was inspired by "freedom versus no freedom" and "entrapment versus release".

Feel free to interpret this piece of music, choose your key and tempo to make it your own and submit it to us via social media, tagging us or send to rosanne@memoriesoflockdown.com
  It would be interesting to see your interpretation! Enjoy!

"Feelings through Lockdown"

Conclusion

"I hope you enjoyed the unique and different stories from my unique and different friends and realise that each story is the heartfelt truth of the person who wrote it even if it is not your truth.

I am grateful every day that my dear parents are not here to witness what is happening and for the strength they give me spiritually now.

I can remember many conversations over the years when we have questioned how long the world could go on "like this". Destruction, Division, Poverty, Wars, Starvation and more. I think we now have our answer and I have a deep knowing that we need to go through what we are going through now.

I believe we - a general "we" not necessarily me or you - will get through this and we will go onto better things but I believe there will be major changes and life will never be the same again.

I am ready and willing to embrace the change and I wake up every morning ready to step forward into another day knowing and trusting that everything is exactly how it's meant to be.

To all my dear friends who joined me in this book "thank you for trusting me".

To all my readers - if you enjoyed this book please look out for Book 2 which will include continuing and new stories. If you want to tell your story in Book 2 please contact me via the website You can find us on **www.memoriesoflockdown.com**

For the many many people across the world suffering hugely in these covid times with depression, illness, lack of medical treatment, loneliness, domestic abuse including children at risk, people losing their businesses and the many many other consequences of these times + ongoing hardships such as starvation, poverty, disease & human & child trafficking - we are collectively praying for you and a better brighter future for us all.

Sending love to you all and may 2022 bring everything we need to start going forward to a much brighter future."

Rosanne ♥ ♥ ♥

Mark Watson - Letter from the Aegean to the North Lands

It's all still here:
the Oleander red and white and blush pink roadsides
the skin warmth of evening walks
the drifting night fragrance from Jasmine stars
a taverna on a well lit street
or quieter still among basil pots in a tucked away alley
under an overspreading roof of purple bougainvillea
And in among the ruins where the tall grasses grow
the poppies peel their red petals
and the pale blue cornflowers open to the bright morning sun

There, on a night time street, at a bar, at the pension door
you meet him or her, and, warmed by the mood of summer
the promise of love flourishes
and all misunderstandings are put on hold

and the next day is spent on a secluded beach
in anticipation of the coming night
and of all those nights to follow
with no thoughts of any future
Yes, it's still here.

So if winter winds and lockdown rains
have you guessing, wondering, testing the memories
maldistanced now
not sure if they are, were ever true
it's all still here
as rich, as real, as vibrant as the violet thyme flower
that, just plucked, burst its flavor onto my tongue
as momentous as a brand new sun bursting through the clouds of
doubt that have masked our memories
and thrown them into the black hole of an almost abandoned past;
the sun still shines on who we all were, and are, and will be again
the message is clear
from this bright hot Aegean beach
from the bluest of skies that rests above it
from the sun that shines the way to a new future
it's all still here.

Will this be the Winter of Discontent?

Topics being discussed as we go to print at the end of September 2021:

Will we have a Winter Lockdown?

Continued discussion on the vaccine:
booster vaccine for those already double jabbed,
vaccine for children,12-15, already being rolled out in schools - with or without parent´s permission
vaccine trials for children under 12, as young as 6 months

Other News Being Discussed:
Energy Crisis - Prices going up
Fuel Shortages
Food Shortages
The end of the £20-a-week boost to Universal Credit could mean many UK households face a "very difficult winter" - will affect 6 million families
Furlough ending
Tax Rises
Bank of England predicting Inflation heading to 4%
Will interest rates go up?
HGV Drivers - not just a UK problem - it´s all over Europe
Are these the after-effects of policy to lock down the economy?